THE
POWER OF
JESUS'
NAMES

TONY EVANS

HARVEST HOUSE PUBLISHERS
EUGENE, OREGON

Cover design by Bryce Williamson

Cover photo © Pearl / Lightstock

The Power of Jesus' Names
Copyright © 2019 by Tony Evans
Published by Harvest House Publishers
Eugene, Oregon 97408
www.harvesthousepublishers.com

ISBN 978-0-7369-6067-0 (pbk.)
ISBN 978-0-7369-6068-7 (eBook)

Library of Congress Cataloging-in-Publication Data

Names: Evans, Tony, 1949- author.
Title: The power of Jesus' names / Tony Evans.
Description: Eugene : Harvest House Publishers, 2019. | Includes
    bibliographical references and index.
Identifiers: LCCN 2019004530 (print) | LCCN 2019004767 (ebook) | ISBN
    9780736960687 (ebook) | ISBN 9780736960670 (pbk.)
Subjects: LCSH: Jesus Christ--Name.
Classification: LCC BT590.N2 (ebook) | LCC BT590.N2 E93 2019 (print) | DDC
    232--dc23
LC record available at https://lccn.loc.gov/2019004530

Printed in the United States of America
          19 20 21 22 23 24 25 26 / BP-GL / 10 9 8 7 6 5 4 3 2 1

CONTENTS

Acknowledgments

I want to thank my friends at Harvest House Publishers for their long-standing partnership in bringing my thoughts, study, and words to print. I particularly want to thank Bob Hawkins for his friendship over the years, as well as his pursuit of excellence in leading his company. I also want to publicly thank Terry Glaspey, Betty Fletcher, and Amber Holcomb for their help in the editorial process. In addition, my appreciation goes out to Heather Hair for her skills and insights in collaboration on this manuscript.

THE CELEBRITYSHIP
OF JESUS

We live in a day of saccharin celebrities and celebrity substitutes. These are people seeking a name through popularity, position, or power. Everyone wants to be recognized. Some of us will even wear a jersey with the name of a sports star on it just to identify with a celebrity, someone we have never met.

Social media has introduced many different forms of celebrityship into our world as well. Now we can feel like we might know the famous because we see their Instagram posts, read their blogs, or listen to their podcasts. It may *seem* like we know them, but we only know what they choose to reveal. Regardless, we can't get enough, and social media has given rise to the phenomenon known as the "instant celebrity." Depending on the number of followers a person has online, he or she can get endorsement deals and much more.

It seems as though we are surrounded by celebrities or celebrity wannabes in our world today. There's a large number of people in our culture whom we are aware of on a very high level, whether due to their talents, sports skills, or social media presence. But the average celebrity's popularity will wane over time, and even if they do manage to keep it for longer than normal and wind up with memorials or parades in their name, most people will only think of them when reading history books, watching the parade, or visiting the memorial.

People with large platforms may look impressive now. Their follower counts may seem enormous. But give it time, and all of that will dissipate.

Yet there is one name that has never passed and will never pass into oblivion—and that's the name of Jesus.

He never published a book, and yet there are more books written about Him than on any other subject. He never wrote a song, and yet there are more songs written about Him than any other person who lived. He never physically traveled more than 300 miles from the place of His birth, and yet there is virtually no place on earth you can go where people do not know His name. Our calendars are set by His entrance into human history. His notoriety only increases with time, although He's been physically gone from earth for more than 2,000 years.

Jesus is a unique celebrity. Stores bank on making a profit the month of His birthday. They know when that day rolls around, they will experience an enormous increase in sales. Family gatherings will take place all around the world in celebration of His resurrection. All four of the Gospels give us the narrative of His birth. And Paul gives us a theological summary on why Jesus is the only candidate for which "celebrity" should rightfully apply in Philippians 2:6-7: "Who, although He existed in the form of God, did not regard equality with God a thing to be grasped, but emptied Himself, taking the form of a bond-servant, and being made in the likeness of men."

Jesus, a unique part of the Godhead, became a slave for us and emptied Himself. Theologians call it the *kenosis*, when deity emptied into humanity. What we had on that first Christmas morning was a baby in a manger who had created His own mother. What we had was a baby in a stable who had created His own stepfather, as well as the donkeys, sheep, and shepherds who surrounded Him. He made the hay on which He lay. He formed the ground on which His bed was set. On the day Jesus entered our earth as a baby, God poured Himself into flesh. He became the most unique human being to ever exist and the only one who is to be given true celebrity status, as the apostle Paul writes in Philippians 2:9-11: "God highly exalted Him, and bestowed on Him the name which is above every name, so that at the name of Jesus every knee will bow, of those who are in heaven and on earth and under the earth, and that every tongue will confess that Jesus Christ is Lord, to the glory of God the Father."

What's more, unlike most celebrities who travel with an entourage and keep others at bay, Jesus has made it possible for us to get to know Him as much as we want. He has made Himself accessible to us. He came that we might have life and know His presence intimately. And knowing Him provides us access to things only a celebrity like Jesus can gain.

As you get to know and understand the various names and

descriptions of Jesus throughout this book and submit yourself to His authority, you will discover how you can tap into
the power of the one and only, the greatest celebrity in the universe: Jesus, your Lord, your Christ, and your God.

PART 1

POWER IN HIS POSITIONS

Behold, a virgin will be with child and bear a son,
and she will call His name Immanuel.

Now all this took place to fulfill what was spoken
by the Lord through the prophet: "Behold, the
virgin shall be with Child and shall bear a Son,
and they shall call His name Immanuel," which
translated means, "God with us."

MATTHEW 1:22-23

1

IMMANUEL

Names matter.

When you say the name of a person, you are speaking of their identity. If you were to approach a group of people whom you know and ask to speak to someone named Avery, it would be Avery who answered. It wouldn't be Chris. The reason why Avery would answer is because that is his name. That is his identity. It is not Chris' identity.

Names are more than nomenclature. Names involve identity. In the Bible, names were often given at the earliest possible time in an effort by the parents to define the hopes and dreams of their child. Thus, the parents would choose a name to reflect what the child was destined to become.

Names matter.

Some names live in infamy. You don't see a parent naming their child Adolf Hitler, Judas, Jezebel, or Benedict Arnold. If they did, most people would question their mental health.

Some might ask, "Why did you name your child this? Don't you know what that name stands for?"

Why? Because names matter.

There are other names that, when spoken, immediately conjure up thoughts reaching far beyond the syllables themselves. If a person mentions Bill Gates, most people think of wealth and success. If you talk about Obama or Trump, you're going to conjure up thoughts about an office and position—and perhaps some strong feelings. If someone brings up Michael Jordan, then basketball and greatness come to mind. This is because a name reflects an identity.

If names matter to us, you can imagine they matter all the more to God—the Creator and originator of humanity, in whose image we have been made.

The various names of God reflect His character and attributes. He refers to Himself throughout Scripture with many different names. Each one draws us into a quality of and relational connection with Him that help us to identify who He is in each particular moment and situation. The variety of His names enables us to get to know Him better, as well as to understand the numerous ways He is able to work both in and through our lives.

Not only does God the Father go by many meaningful names, but Jesus—God the Son—has a number of names Himself. Before we dive deeply into any of them, let's spend a moment setting the stage. You're invited to take a seat as the curtain is drawn and the first scene begins, revealing and welcoming Jesus into the world.

Let's direct our attention back to about 2,000 years ago.

A Unique Birth

A new birth in a royal family usually comes with great pomp and fanfare. There is massive media saturation and a lot of celebration. But not in the case of Jesus. He came as a king, and He could have been born in a castle. Yet the babe was born in a barn to parents who were both unknown and poor, and He arrived with little worldly notice. Nobody sent flowers. No nursemaid helped with his diapers. The few gifts He received would come much later.

Why should we even give attention to Jesus? Because heaven's own heart had beat in the womb of a young woman for the previous nine months. Most likely just a young teenager herself, Jesus' mother, Mary, was full of a faith far greater than the years she had known. Out of her body came God's omnipotence covered in humanity's limitations.

Her child was flesh, bones, sinew, and blood. Yet He was also the perfection of deity. He felt hunger because He was fully human, yet He would later feed five thousand because He was fully God (Luke 9:10-17). He grew thirsty because He was fully human, yet He would one day walk on water because He was fully God (John 6:16-21). Raised by a peasant girl and a carpenter, He grew in knowledge (Luke 2:52), yet He also knew what others thought (Matthew 9:3-4).

Jesus' birth was like no other, for in Him, God took on human flesh. Deity was wearing a diaper.

But how did a virgin have a baby?

If anyone knew about the difficulties surrounding a virgin birth, it was Luke. Luke, the writer of the Gospel bearing his name, was a physician by trade and a Greek by culture. His mind was committed to details, data, and order. His writings reflect organization and careful research. No hint of fairy tale, myth, or fable surrounds his words. Luke was a scholar and an intellect. If anyone should know that a virgin cannot give birth, it would be a doctor. Yet it was a doctor who wrote of the virgin birth as fluidly as if taking down notes on a patient's chart.

Patient: Mary

History: Virgin

Status: Mother

When I go to the doctor, I usually have a written list of questions I want to ask. You also might make a list; after all, it's not every day we have the opportunity to talk with a doctor. On top of that, a doctor's time is usually rushed. I've found that if I don't have my questions prepared and written, I'll go through my appointment, get out to my car, and then remember that one important thing I had intended to ask.

Having likely dealt with his own patients throughout years of practice, Luke probably grew to anticipate questions as well. Considering the uniqueness of Mary's situation, he might have known that most people would ask how a virgin could have a baby. Maybe that's why he chose to make the point so clear from the start.

Twice in Luke 1:26-33, Luke used the word *virgin*. Twice he drew attention to the single detail that's critical to everything else. Twice he piqued our interest with such a seemingly obvious contradiction. After all, everyone knows that a virgin can't have a baby!

Luke's emphasis highlights God's role in this event. This was no ordinary conception. Don't miss that. Without this distinction, Mary's child would have been like everyone else's. Yet in this one unique conception and birth, the immaterial and the material merged. Nobility entered poverty. Divine holiness combined with humanity. God became human.

Matthew wasn't a doctor, but in his Gospel, he gave another testimony to highlight the virgin birth. In our Lord's genealogy, he wrote, "Jacob fathered Joseph the husband of Mary, who gave birth to Jesus who is called the Messiah" (Matthew 1:16 HCSB).

The first *who* is important in this verse. It is a feminine singular relative pronoun in the Greek. Now, don't get tripped up by all those terms. Basically, what the language tells us is that Jesus was conceived through Mary, but not by Joseph. In other words, Joseph was Mary's husband, but he wasn't Jesus' father. Jesus was conceived by the Holy Spirit so that His human nature might be sinless. His humanity had both a heavenly origin through the power of God's Spirit and an earthly origin through Mary. The virgin birth thus circumvented the transfer of a sinful nature.

The angel Gabriel had been sent by God to communicate the circumstances of Jesus' conception and birth to Mary. It was certainly unique to have an angelic visit, and his words were even more unusual. But, as Gabriel said, none of this should cause fear in Mary because "the Lord is with you" (see Luke 1:28,30).

Gabriel went on to make Mary aware of the special role Jesus would play in history—and for all eternity. "He will be

great and will be called the Son of the Most High; and the
Lord God will give Him the throne of His father David; and
He will reign over the house of Jacob forever, and His king-
dom will have no end" (verses 32-33).

As Messiah and King over all, Jesus has already established
the rules of His reign. He has set the tone through His life. In
His kingdom, neither race nor gender nor wealth nor social
status determines our place in Him (Galatians 3:28). Christ
gives strength to the weak who recognize their weakness and
look to Him. Forgiveness trumps bitterness, and the amount
of money you have (or don't have) doesn't matter; what matters is the heart. Significance in Jesus' kingdom is tied to service (John 13:12-17).

The baby born of the virgin, laid in the soft hay of a manger, came not only to live and die, but to reign in power and
glory. Through Jesus, the God of heaven has set up a kingdom
that will never be destroyed nor left to another people (Daniel
2:44). His kingdom and reign will last forever.

Mary did not doubt the announcement from Gabriel, but
she did ask a question: "How?" (see Luke 1:34). She didn't
question God's power or ability, but she wondered how He
would accomplish the miraculous.

Gabriel's response is rich with meaning: "The Holy Spirit
will come upon you, and the power of the Most High will
overshadow you" (verse 35). Ponder that statement in light of
other Scriptures.

"A child will be born to us, a son will be given to us" (Isaiah
9:6). Notice that one word: *given*. The Son was given by God.
As the Son of God, Jesus already existed, but He came to earth

through human birth. That's why it could be said of Him that He created the universe. Too many people want to keep Jesus in the manger because they don't want to deal with His deity. As long as they can keep Him asleep in the stable, they don't have to reckon with the reality that He's God on a throne. But He was already God. Thus, the Son had to be "given."

"When the time came to completion, God sent His Son, born of a woman, born under the law" (Galatians 4:4 HCSB). Paul highlighted the reality of deity merging with humanity. God sent His Son—the Son was "given"—yet Jesus was "born of a woman." God became a man. This verse clearly summarizes the incarnation of Jesus Christ.

The two natures of Jesus Christ form what theologians call the *hypostatic union*. If you don't know what that means, it's just a big term that simply refers to the reality that Jesus is made up of undiminished deity and perfect humanity. He became no less God when He became human. Mary did not give birth to both God and a man. Jesus was not 50 percent human and 50 percent God. Rather, Mary gave birth to the God-man—God with us, Immanuel. We read in Colossians 1:19 that "God was pleased to have all His fullness dwell in Him" (HCSB).

The Bible often equates Jesus with God, reinforcing this relationship. Genesis 1:1 tells us that God created the world, and Colossians 1:16 tells us that all things were created by Christ Jesus. So, either we have two creators, or the God of Genesis 1:1 is also the God of Colossians 1:16. Jesus Christ is distinct from God the Father in His person, yet equal with the Father in His deity. He took on human flesh, being born as a baby in a world of darkness. He came for the purpose of making the invisible God visible to us in history.

Jesus' birth was a birth like no other because He is like no other. Jesus came to earth as the Son of God so that we may know God and experience Him more fully. That was His entrance. That was His birth. It was truly like no other. Why? Because Jesus is like no other. And one of the ways you and I can get to know Jesus more fully and the power He offers to give us in our daily lives is through coming to understand His names and how He chose to reveal Himself to us on earth.

See, Jesus could have come to a castle and portrayed Himself to be king. But then most of us who are from the common realms of life would never have been able to identify with Him. Rather, Jesus was born in a barn in the insignificant village of Bethlehem. There was no bed for His head. His parents were poor, young, and unknown. The society into which He came was one of chaos. That's a life many of us can relate to. We can somehow identify with His struggle, lack, and loss. We can feel like He's "one of our own."

God gave us a Savior we could understand. In understanding Him and getting to know His names, we get to know and understand God all the more as well. John 1:18 says, "No one has ever seen God; the only God, who is at the Father's side, he has made him known" (ESV).

If anybody comes to you claiming to have seen God, you're looking at either a liar or a confused individual. The Scripture says no one has seen God. Flimsy human bodies were never constructed to stand in the presence of His glory. It's like staring straight into the sun. It can't and shouldn't be done. There's too much power for a direct stare.

So how could God fully reveal Himself without vaporizing us? Answer: He is fully revealed in Jesus. To understand Jesus is to understand God.

Philip had been one of Jesus' disciples for almost three years when he came up with an interesting request. "Show us the Father," he said, "and it is enough for us" (John 14:8). Jesus' answer puts His purpose in perspective. "Have I been so long with you, and yet you have not come to know Me, Philip? He who has seen Me has seen the Father" (verse 9).

Jesus took everything there was to know about God and put it on a shelf we could reach. Jesus is the complete revelation of God. That's why you can't bypass Jesus and get to God. You can't skip Jesus and have God. You can't deny Jesus and know God. Jesus is the only begotten Son—the only one. Jesus is *God with us*. He is Immanuel.

God with Us

A master key is designed to unlock multiple doors—and Jesus is our master key to God Himself. He reveals to us the heart and mind and nature of God. It is through Jesus that we get to know God. It is through Jesus that we come to discover the depth of His power. It is through Jesus that we understand the fullness of His love. Without Jesus, we would never have gained entrance into the presence of God. Not only that, but we would also be limited in our understanding of His full character.

No other name of Jesus reflects the nature of God's heart

toward us like the name Immanuel, which is why I've chosen
to start with it. We see this name in Matthew 1:22-23, and it
sets the stage for all the names to follow.

> All this took place to fulfill what was spoken by
> the Lord through the prophet: "Behold, the vir-
> gin shall be with child and shall bear a Son, and
> they shall call His name Immanuel," which trans-
> lated means, "God with us."

The meaning of Immanuel is given to us right in the passage: "God with us." Yet the context of that meaning can only
be found in Isaiah, which Matthew referenced here. During
the time of Isaiah's writing about Immanuel, God's people
were being attacked by the enemy. They stared disaster in the
face. The king could see no sure way to victory for himself or
his nation. It was in the midst of this fear, anxiety, and dread
that God showed up and told King Ahaz that He would give
him a sign of victory. This would be no ordinary sign either. A
virgin would bear a son (see Isaiah 7:1-14).

It was prophesied that when this sign came about, there
would be victory. It was also promised that when this sign
came about, it would be an ongoing reminder of God's presence with them, in spite of what was attacking them.

The name Immanuel originated within a context of pain,
despair, loss, doubt, fear, and chaos. Immanuel came to
a world in crisis. It is not merely a name to remember during Christmas as we sing carols and drink hot chocolate. No,
Immanuel is a name of comfort when times are at their worst.

One of the first things you need to understand about Jesus

is that no matter what you have gone through or are currently going through, He is with you. No matter how difficult the challenges you face, God is with you. No matter how many enemies attack you—whether internally or externally—God is with you. Whatever you are facing, struggling with, enduring, or exhausted from, God is with you. The birth of Jesus Christ is not only the introduction of our Savior into this world; it is also the introduction of God's promise of victory and His presence in the midst of a painful reality we all know far too well.

Friend, God is with you. Jesus came that we may know God more fully and experience His power more completely as He deals with our sins and our circumstances.

This is one of the primary things I want you to understand as we begin our look at Jesus' names. No matter what you have gone through, you are not alone. No matter what difficulties have threatened to drown you, you can overcome. No matter what challenges you are facing—however big or small—God's victory is in your grasp because His presence is with you. You are not facing anything on your own.

When Matthew introduced the name Immanuel by referring back to Isaiah, he reminded his readers, who were suffering under Roman oppression, of the prophecy's context. He assured them of the presence of God in a decaying and challenging season. He emphasized that this entry of Immanuel into our world was a reminder that God is with each of us—even, and especially, when things are not in our favor. Jesus gives us God in the flesh. Colossians 1:15 puts it this way: "He is the image of the invisible God, the firstborn of all creation." He is "the exact representation" of God (Hebrews 1:3).

When we talk about Jesus—Immanuel—we are talking about God Himself. We are not just talking about a man who lived and died on earth. This is God in the flesh. Over and over again in Scripture, we witness Jesus manifesting the fullness of deity, which is God alone. Even when it comes to the names of God, Jesus exemplifies and embodies them. Let's look at a few examples of "God with us."

- In the Old Testament, God is called *Elohim*, which means the Creator God. The New Testament tells us that everything has been created by Jesus (Colossians 1:16).

- God is also known as *Jehovah*, the great I Am. When Jesus came, He said, "Before Abraham was born, I am" (John 8:58).

- We know God as *Jehovah Nissi*, which means He is our banner of victory. In the New Testament, Jesus said He has "overcome the world" (John 16:33).

- One of God's names is *Jehovah Rohi*, which means that the Lord is our shepherd. Jesus came to us as the good shepherd whose sheep know His voice (John 10:4,11).

- God is called *Jehovah Sabaoth*. This name refers to Him as the Lord of hosts. Jesus said that He could have called 12 legions of angels to fight on His behalf; He commands the armies of heaven (Matthew 26:53).

- Another name of God is *El Elyon*, meaning the Lord who is high and mighty. Jesus sits at the right hand of the Father, high above (Ephesians 1:20-21).

- A very popular name of God in our culture today is *El Shaddai*, which means God Almighty. Scripture speaks of Jesus in the same terms when it says that Jesus Christ is Lord Almighty (Revelation 1:8).

Jesus is God with us in every way. If you want to get to know the names of Jesus, just get to know the names of God, because Jesus is the fulfillment of every name of God. And He has come as Immanuel, "God with us," in order to reveal God to us. Should you ever become confused about who God is and what He is like, all you have to do is remember Immanuel.

Why did God send Immanuel to us, rather than just reveal Himself as He is? God is transcendent in nature. He sits outside our realm. He is infinitely distinct from His creation—in another zone. And yet, God wanted to be with us. He desired to dwell among us. And this could only occur through the hypostatic union, through the merging of two natures into one person (Jesus) that remain unmixed forever. Jesus is both divine and human, which is why Jesus can be called both the Son of God and the Son of Man.

Hebrews 10:5-7 gives insight into the purpose and plan of Immanuel:

> When Christ came into the world, he said: "Sacrifice and offering you did not desire, but a body you prepared for me; with burnt offerings and sin offerings you were not pleased. Then I said, 'Here

I am—it is written about me in the scroll—I have
come to do your will, my God'" (NIV).

First, Jesus said, "Sacrifice and offering you did not
desire…with burnt offerings and sin offerings you were not
pleased"—though they were offered in accordance with the
law. Second, He said, "Here I am…I have come to do your
will." He sets aside the first to establish the second.

The incarnation came to be in order that the Father's will
would be carried out. A perfect sacrifice was made for the sins
of humanity. And in the midst of that incarnational gift, we
discover that God placed Himself into a context where we
could come to know Him in a more personal, intimate way.

He is "God with us." He is God with *you*.

From the beginning of the world to its end, there is no
place you can look and not see God revealed through Jesus.
He is everywhere. Colossians 1:17 summarizes the breadth and
magnitude of Him better than any other verse: "He is before
all things, and in Him all things hold together."

Choosing Immanuel

There's an oft-told story of a wealthy man who had lost his
beloved son, and then later he himself died. Over the course
of his life, he had accumulated a number of expensive, valu-
able, and rare commodities, which, following his death, were
to be auctioned off in an estate sale. Knowing of the man's
taste in exquisite furniture, art, and the like, hundreds of people showed up for this auction.

The day began, though, with a piece that most showed no

interest in at all. The auctioneer came forward with a cheaply framed picture, saying, "The first piece we're offering today is this portrait of the man's only son." He paused to give everyone a chance to view it, then continued, "Do I have a bid?"

The room fell silent, as no one raised their hand to bid on this framed portrait. They had come for some of the expensive art pieces and artifacts, not for something as simple as that. The auctioneer stood still, not saying a word—something auctioneers are rarely seen doing—but he could tell by the expressions on the faces of the attendees that this wasn't something anyone really wanted to buy. Still, he asked once more, "Do I have a bid? Does anyone want this portrait of the man's son?"

Just then, from the back of the room, an elderly man stepped forward and said, "Sir, I was the servant of the man who died, and if nobody will take the picture of his son, I want to know if I can have it."

The auctioneer said, "One more time. Is there anyone who will bid on the picture of the son?" Yet nobody did. So he said to the servant, "Yes, sir, the picture is yours."

The elderly servant slowly walked forward to take hold of the portrait. Looking lovingly on the boy's image, he then tucked it under his arm and headed toward the back of the room. To everyone's shock, the auctioneer then picked up his gavel, banged it down, and said, "The auction is now over."

Everybody looked around, and someone said, "What? You haven't brought out any of the expensive pieces that were supposed to be sold. How can the auction be over?"

The auctioneer replied, "The father's will says that the

auction was to begin with the picture of his son. He valued his son so highly that he stipulated that whoever took his son's picture would inherit everything."

Essentially, he who has the son has everything else. He who does not have the son gets nothing.

Sometimes we are like those buyers at the estate auction. We're going around looking for everything else to buy, but God is there saying, "I have come to give you life and to give it to you more abundantly. But that life can only be found in connection with My Son. If you have My Son, you have eternal life and all that goes with it." Scripture states this clearly for us in the book of Romans, where we read, "He who did not spare His own Son, but delivered Him over for us all, how will He not also with Him freely give us all things?" (8:32).[1]

When you abide with Jesus, you will gain access to all that God the Father has for you. And knowing and understanding Jesus' names gives you insight on how to abide more fully in Him. Let's get to know Jesus, Immanuel, as we should and, in so doing, tap into the power He longs to supply (John 10:10).

*Thus says the LORD, the King of Israel and his
Redeemer, the LORD of hosts: "I am the first and I
am the last, and there is no God besides Me."*

ISAIAH 44:6

*Behold, I am coming quickly, and My reward is
with Me, to render to every man according to what
he has done. I am the Alpha and Omega, the first
and the last, the beginning and the end.*

REVELATION 22:12-13

2

ALPHA AND OMEGA

What better place to continue looking at the names of Jesus than the beginning? *Alpha* is the very first letter in the Greek alphabet. It is also one of the names of Jesus. But before we get to it, let's look at the English alphabet first.

One of the first things we were taught when we started school, or even before then, was the alphabet. Parents, grandparents, and teachers seek to teach young children the alphabet as early as their first year of life. When I was growing up, we had songs that helped us memorize it. Today, there are a variety of games, toys, and videos little ones can interact with that will help them learn not only the letters, but also the sounds of each letter.

The reason why learning the alphabet is such an emphasized part of childhood is because knowing A to Z serves as the foundation upon which we can understand all words. Words depend on letters. Letters make up words. These words then comprise our thoughts, and the communication of those thoughts becomes the bedrock for all knowledge.

Imagine what your life would look like if you didn't know the alphabet. You would not be able to read. You would not be able to communicate clearly. You would not know how to juxtapose consonants and vowels so that pronunciation could be accurate and clear. You would find yourself in a world of hurt trying to live in your part of the world without a knowledge of the English alphabet.

Now, you still may have had some experience in this. Perhaps you've visited a foreign country and didn't speak the language. Understanding simple things in that situation is nearly impossible. Try asking for directions in English in a country where the language is not spoken. It's doubtful you'll wind up at your desired location. Why? Because accurate communication rests on an accurate understanding and application of the building blocks of a language.

Because we know how important language and words are, we will often use the phrase "from A to Z" to indicate the fullness of a task or topic. This isn't merely referring to the letters in the alphabet. Rather, this phrase references the completeness of whatever point is being made.

The reason why the alphabet is so critical is because letters matter, words matter, thoughts matter, and knowledge matters.

Now, what "A to Z" is in the English language, "alpha and omega" is in Greek. *Alpha* is the first letter of the Greek alphabet, and *omega* is the last. When Jesus lived on earth, He lived in a Greek-speaking world. He understood the significance of *alpha* and *omega*. Just as "A to Z" signifies the completeness of communication, fullness of knowledge, and clarity of thought, the phrase "alpha and omega" symbolized the same for the culture in which Jesus lived. Thus, when He says He is the Alpha and the Omega, He is declaring that He Himself is the complete knowledge base for all life. He is the entirety of all information. He is the answer to all questions. He is the sufficiency of all communication. He is the sum total of all that can be totaled.

Jesus followed up His claim to the name of Alpha and Omega by further identifying the scope of His existence and being. He did this by adding that He is "the first and the last" (Revelation 22:13). Essentially, no letter comes before Him, and no letter comes after Him. He is the first, the last, and everything in between. Not only that, but by saying this, He also declared that He is the living God. We know this because God referred to Himself in the same way in the Old Testament.

In Isaiah 44:6, we read, "Thus says the LORD, the King of Israel and his Redeemer, the LORD of hosts: 'I am the first and I am the last, and there is no God besides Me.'" And Isaiah 48:12 says, "Listen to Me, O Jacob, even Israel whom I called; I am He, I am the first, I am also the last."

When Jesus declared He is the Alpha and the Omega, the first and the last, He declared that He is the God of the Old Testament. This name, in particular, is a claim to deity. It is an acknowledgment of divinity. Because, after all, how many firsts or lasts can there be? If the God of the Old Testament introduced His identity as being the first and the last, then when Jesus described Himself in the same manner, He was revealing that He is a part of the Godhead.

Jesus Is the Final Word

In addition to proclaiming His divine nature through the name Alpha and Omega, Jesus also made clear that He is the complete manifestation of all that is to be known about God. This is because letters form words, and words express thoughts, and He has placed Himself as the sum total of all the letters that make up the alphabet. Jesus has complete information as God and conveys all there is to be known of God.

This means that if someone comes up with their own version of truth or their own understanding of God apart from Jesus' revelation and manifestation of God, they are wrong. There is no right way to create a word in the English language apart from utilizing the letters of the English alphabet. If someone creates a word not using the letters of the English alphabet, then that word will not be an English word. Similarly, Jesus has made it clear that He is the totality of all the letters from *alpha* to *omega*. Nothing can be created within Jesus' realm that doesn't proceed from Him as the root. It simply won't be true.

The theology derived from this particular name of Jesus can be summarized in that He is the complete totality of all knowledge on any subject, as well as the full revelation of God Himself. There is no subject matter that sits outside Jesus. All wisdom and knowledge is rooted in Him. Problems arise in our lives when we do not take this name seriously.

When we view Jesus as a great historical figure who healed people and did good, but we do not allow Him to inform every aspect of our lives, we lack the wisdom and knowledge to make productive and healthy choices. Far too many believers give Jesus a nod on Sundays but do not look to Him as the ruler over all. Which is why far too many believ ers struggle just to get by, rather than live out the abundant life Jesus died to provide.

Jesus isn't the A to G in our lives. He isn't to be taken into consideration some of the time. He is the ultimate Alpha and Omega, the beginning and the end. He is over all. Repeatedly in Scripture, we read about the comprehensive nature and rule of Christ. Following are a few examples.

- *Ephesians 1:9-10*—"He has made known to us the mystery of His will, according to His kind intention which He purposed in Him with a view to an administration suitable to the fullness of the times, that is, the summing up of all things in Christ, things in the heavens and things on the earth."

- *Ephesians 1:21*—"Far above all rule and authority and power and dominion, and every name that is named, not only in this age but also in the one to come."

- *Colossians 1:15*—"He is the image of the invisible God, the firstborn of all creation."

- *Colossians 1:17*—"He is before all things, and in Him all things hold together."

- *Colossians 1:19*—"It was the Father's good pleasure for all the fullness to dwell in Him."

- *Colossians 2:3*—"In whom are hidden all the treasures of wisdom and knowledge."

- *Colossians 2:9*—"In Him all the fullness of Deity dwells in bodily form."

- *Colossians 3:11*—"A renewal in which there is no distinction between Greek and Jew, circumcised and uncircumcised, barbarian, Scythian, slave and freeman, but Christ is all, and in all."

Did you notice a repeated word in those verses? That word is *all*. Jesus knows all. Jesus understands all. Jesus embodies all. Jesus rules over all. Thus, what you or I think on any subject matter is irrelevant when it doesn't agree with Him. Any knowledge that disagrees with Jesus is polluted and ignorant. No matter what your friends think—or the media, analysts, or even professors and speakers—whenever these individuals differ from the truth found in Jesus Christ, they are wrong. It's very plain and simple. When a person abdicates the knowledge of God, they will discover that human wisdom leads to a road pitted with pain, disappointment, and emptiness.

Friend, God has spoken, and He has not stuttered. There are two answers to every question: God's answer, and everybody else's. And when everybody else disagrees with God, everybody else is wrong. James 3:15 says that human wisdom is the thinking of demons. It's not just foolishness; it is evil.

Spiritual wisdom, on the other hand, includes the ability to use knowledge correctly. Knowledge is information. Wisdom is the ability to use that information for a positive impact and outcome. See, a person can have knowledge while possessing little, or no, wisdom. That's why people can actually become "educated fools," because even though they possess multiple degrees, they might not know how to apply that knowledge in a wise way. When a person doesn't know what to do with the information they have in order to make right decisions in life, that person will run into a variety of consequences that will rob them of their peace and power.

Hebrews 12:25 tells us that we are not to "refuse Him who is speaking." We are not to turn away from what Jesus says. And while most of us would deny we do that or dismiss the level to which we do, it is a common occurrence in Christendom to not take Jesus' words seriously. His cross is a great ornament to have up on the wall or around our necks. You can't walk into a gas station or convenience store in the Bible Belt states and not run straight into an array of jeweled or stone crosses available in every size. And while remembering Jesus' atonement is something we should do, remembering and applying His words is just as critical. What good is a cross hanging on the wall or a Bible sitting on a coffee table in a home where the inhabitants don't even take the time to find out what Jesus has said?

Obey Jesus based on what He has said. The cross becomes no more than a symbolic charm if we're not abiding in the Word of the one who is the summation of all knowledge and wisdom. In fact, God tells us that when we do not listen to His Son and apply His truth, He will shake up our lives in order to get our attention (see Hebrews 12:10-11). And in

Hebrews 1:2, we read, "In these last days [God] has spoken to us in His Son, whom He appointed heir of all things, through whom also He made the world." Thus, Jesus is not just the final word on religion or spiritual matters. Rather, He is the final word on all things, whether it be marriage, money, parenting, work, heaven, hell, entertainment, relationships, or anything else. He's the final word on it all. And it all points back to Him. First Corinthians 15:27-28 tells us:

> He has put all things in subjection under His feet. But when He says, "All things are put in subjection," it is evident that He is excepted who put all things in subjection to Him. When all things are subjected to Him, then the Son Himself also will be subjected to the One who subjected all things to Him, so that God may be all in all.

To paraphrase C.S. Lewis, I believe in the sun not just because I see it, but because I see everything else because of it.[2] Similarly, we are not just to believe in Jesus, but we are to view everything in life through the lens of His perspective.

Every single part of your life and mind is to be connected, plugged into, and in sync with Jesus Christ. He is the revelation of God from heaven to earth. His job was and is to bring the truth of heaven to bear on our lives on earth. What Jesus says, goes. At least that's how it should be.

Perhaps your parents or guardians used to say to you when you were busy complaining or arguing as a kid, "Didn't you hear what I said?" Maybe you've said that to your kids. The bottom line is that the final word has been said, and the topic is no longer up for discussion.

Jesus is the final word. Period.

Some of our meetings last too long. Some of our discussions last too long. Some of our arguments last too long. And the reason they last too long is that Jesus is not acknowledged as the Alpha and the Omega, the beginning and the end, on all truth. We don't start with Him. We tend to come to Him only when we need Him to bail us out. But that's not who He is. That's not why He came.

Jesus came so that we might have life and have it to the full capacity (John 10:10), but that only happens when we align our lives under His overarching truth. We tap into His strength when we tap into His truth. We grasp His peace when we grasp His truth. We enjoy His provision when we employ His truth. This is a cause-and-effect relationship, dependent upon our understanding and application of the Word of God as embodied in the life of Jesus Christ.

Finishing Strong

What can a person accomplish who discovers the secret of aligning their lives under Jesus' truth? This person can finish the race and fulfill the calling God has created them to live out. Hebrews 12:1-3 explains this:

> Since we have so great a cloud of witnesses surrounding us, let us also lay aside every encumbrance and the sin which so easily entangles us, and let us run with endurance the race that is set before us, fixing our eyes on Jesus, the author and perfecter of faith, who for the joy set before Him endured the cross, despising the shame, and has sat down at the right hand of the throne of God.

> For consider Him who has endured such hostil-
> ity by sinners against Himself, so that you will not
> grow weary and lose heart.

Friend, I understand that you are probably tired right now. In Scripture, this type of tired is known as being "weary" or "losing heart." Life may not be working in your favor, as you see it. Sure, it could be your fault why it hasn't. But it could also be someone else's fault. Or it could be a combination of both. Regardless of the reason, the result is the same: You are tired. You are worn out. Your hope has waned, and your fervency has fizzled. But what the author of Hebrews is trying to tell you in this passage is that if you are tired, you still need to keep going.

Even though things are rough right now, don't quit.

You have a race to finish—a figurative race of living the kingdom life for the glory of God and the good of yourself and others. And even though you may have gotten sidelined along the way or detoured by heeding human wisdom, Jesus can set you back on that racetrack and help you finish strong.

The author of Hebrews knew he wasn't writing to perfect people. He was writing to people marred by sin and failure and filled with regret. Flawed people who were just plain tired and wanted to quit. He knew all that, which is why he prodded them and goaded them to keep on going. And how were they (and you) to do that? By fixing their eyes on the one who knows how to both start and finish things—the Alpha and the Omega, the beginning and the end.

You have the power to keep going because Jesus has the power to both start and finish whatever it is you might face. He is the origin and completion of your faith walk. What you need to do is change your focus. You need to get back on track. Run the race set before you. And the way you do that is by focusing your eyes on Jesus. Become fixated with Him.

When you are fixated with something or someone, that means you stop being fixated with anything else. It's not possible to be fixated on multiple things at the same time. To be fixated on Jesus means you are zeroing in on Him. You are canceling out all other views. You are no longer looking to other people and their opinions or even your own personal viewpoints. Rather, you are looking at Jesus and Him alone.

Where you look will determine where you go. If you are looking at the mess you are in right now and fixating on everything that is wrong, then you will only continue to walk into more mess. You have to see the way out. You have to look to the power that can overcome.

A great biblical illustration of this is found in Matthew 14:22-31. In this passage, we read about the time when a great storm hit the sea, and yet Jesus walked to His disciples on the rough water. Jesus had sent them out into the bad weather. The problem was the storm. But when Jesus came to the disciples, He walked on top of the very problem itself. Without getting rid of the storm, He overcame it. He overpowered it.

Peter was only able to overcome it himself when he kept his eyes fixed on Jesus. He asked if he could come out on the water too, and as long as he looked at Jesus, he was fine. But when he took his eyes off Jesus and focused instead on the tumultuous circumstances that surrounded him, Peter began to sink.

Friend, whatever you are facing, if you focus on the

circumstances, the circumstances will overwhelm you. They will overpower you. They will swallow you up. Jesus bids you to come to Him in the midst of risky situations. He asks you to step out in faith. But He gives you success only when you keep your eyes focused on Him. You will become consumed by your circumstances if you choose to focus on them. Like Peter, you will sink. But if you choose to return your gaze to Jesus as Peter did, He can lift you back up so you are above the stormy sea once again. Remember, Jesus hadn't moved when Peter started to sink. Peter's focus moved. Only when Peter adjusted his focus back on Jesus did he receive the divine intervention he desperately needed.

Sometimes you might feel like you cannot find God when you are struggling with trials in your life. But God hasn't moved. Rather, your gaze has moved off Him. You need to ask yourself in those times when you cannot feel God's presence or find His peace, "Where are my spiritual eyes directed? What am I looking at?"

When Peter remembered to refocus on Jesus, then Jesus reached down and saved him. He didn't suddenly make the storm go away. He didn't immediately make the winds stop howling. But He did give Peter the ability to rise above the storm and the waves so he could walk with Him back to the security of the boat, and they could all head to shore.

In Philippians 1:6, Paul tells us, "I am confident of this very thing, that He who began a good work in you will perfect it until the day of Christ Jesus." Friend, that's good news! If you come to Jesus, you have come to both the beginning and the end of all that you need. If you focus on Him, He can take you to the finish line.

In the sport of rowing, one member of the team is called the coxswain. This is the person who sits in the stern of the boat. The individuals who do the rowing face backward from the direction they are headed. They cannot see where they are going. All they can see is the coxswain. This person dictates and guides the rowers' cadence. If they were to turn around or take their attention off the coxswain, they would lose time—and in a race, every moment matters. Only when the rowers fix their gaze and attention on the one calling the shots do they have the opportunity of winning.

Life is uncertain. Storms arise. Hardships come at us from too many directions. Yet when we choose to focus our gaze on Jesus Christ and live in cadence with His calling, He will guide us to where we need to go. Keep your eyes on Jesus by seeking His perspective first and communicating with Him on every subject and event in your life. He is the Alpha and the Omega. He is the beginning and the end. He is the author and the finisher, and He will get you across the finish line.

Rejoice greatly, O daughter of Zion!
Shout in triumph, O daughter of Jerusalem!
Behold, your king is coming to you;
He is just and endowed with salvation,
Humble, and mounted on a donkey.

ZECHARIAH 9:9

And on His robe and on His thigh He has a name
written, "KING OF KINGS, AND
LORD OF LORDS."

REVELATION 19:16

3

KING

If you were to come over to my home and ring the door-
bell, and I opened the door to see you smoking a cigarette, I
would ask you to put the cigarette out before coming into my
home. I don't have ashtrays, nor do I let anyone smoke in my
home. So I would not be able or willing to facilitate what you
brought with you.

If you came to my home and started cussing like a sailor, I
would ask you to adjust your language because I do not allow
profanity in my home either. If you came over with your girl-
friend or guy friend and had been invited to stay the night with
us, you could not sleep in the same room or the same bed. I
would show both of you to two separate rooms because, in my
house, no matter what you do in your own home, you would
not be able to share a bedroom. Or do drugs. Or drink strong
alcohol. You get the point.

The reason why you would not be able to do those things

is because you'd be in my house. And in my house, there are certain governing guidelines by which all who enter must adjust.

Maybe in your house you smoke cigarettes, swear, or drink Jack Daniel's. But that wouldn't matter much to me when you came over to my home. Since I pay the mortgage on my house and I pay the bills for my house, it's my domain. Thus, you would have to adjust to my rules. If you fail to adjust, we are going to have a conflict. And even though I may have invited you over, it may not be a meaningful get-together—or a long one—because I will simply ask you to leave if you choose not to abide by my rules.

My daughter Chrystal has a very strong heart and mind. She knows what she wants to do, and that strength has given her the ability to go far in her life, despite challenges and difficulties. But when she was younger and still living at home, that strength sometimes collided with my own. One day she came to me arguing about something, and the argument went on for some time. Seeing that I wouldn't relent on my stand, she decided to walk away while I was still talking to her. I quickly asked, "Where do you think you are going?"

She replied, "I'm going to my room!"

To which I said, "You are not going to your room because that is not your room. That is my room, and I let you sleep in it. And right now, you cannot go there."

See, Chrystal had a wrong view of the room she used in my house. She didn't own it; she got to use it. If you are a parent, then you probably can relate to this. As the parent, you pay the bills and provide the electricity, gas, food, and furniture. And yet your teenagers often want to argue about your rules. They want you to adjust to their rules, but it is your house. Good parenting doesn't adjust. Good parenting establishes loving guidelines and boundaries, which then teaches the children respect, self-control, and obedience.

Friend, we may all understand parenting pretty well. But somewhere along the way, we've forgotten these principles as they relate to God. But God has a house. The name of His house is called His kingdom. God's kingdom is His comprehensive rule over all creation. Psalm 24:1 tells us, "The earth is the LORD's, and all it contains, the world, and those who dwell in it."

God calls His creation His abode. Because it's His abode, He gets to run His house the way He wants to. He makes the rules. If you want to make your own rules, then you need to go make your own world. In this one, God rules. And He has chosen to rule through humanity by entrusting us with the responsibility of stewarding—or managing—His home. I call His rule the *kingdom agenda*, and it forms the basis of everything I teach. The kingdom agenda can be defined as the visible manifestation of the comprehensive rule of God over every area of life. Basically, it involves our alignment underneath the overarching rulership of God. Within that alignment under Him, He has appointed us to have certain responsibilities. We can see this outlined in Scripture:

- *Genesis 1:1*—"In the beginning God created the heavens and the earth."

- *Genesis 2:7*—"Then the LORD God formed man of

dust from the ground, and breathed into his nostrils the breath of life; and man became a living being."

- *Genesis 2:15*—"Then the LORD God took the man and put him into the garden of Eden to cultivate it and keep it."

- *Genesis 1:26-28*—"Then God said, 'Let Us make man in Our image, according to Our likeness; and let them rule over the fish of the sea and over the birds of the sky and over the cattle and over all the earth, and over every creeping thing that creeps on the earth.' God created man in His own image, in the image of God He created him; male and female He created them. God blessed them; and God said to them, 'Be fruitful and multiply, and fill the earth, and subdue it; and rule over the fish of the sea and over the birds of the sky and over every living thing that moves on the earth.'"

- *Psalm 8:4-6*—"What is man that You take thought of him, and the son of man that You care for him? Yet You have made him a little lower than God, and You crown him with glory and majesty! You make him to rule over the works of Your hands; You have put all things under his feet."

- *Psalm 115:16*—"The heavens are the heavens of the LORD, but the earth He has given to the sons of men."

God created an earth-bound creature—a human—whose job was to run His house His way. Yet Adam fumbled that ball early in the game, and he did so decisively. In fumbling, Adam turned the running of the earth over to the devil. When Adam rebelled against the owner of creation, he turned the management of that creation over to Satan by allowing sin to enter the world. This then ushered in chaos, disorder, corruption, and pain.

In order to reinstate humanity's rule, God had to provide another Adam, known as the "last Adam" or "second man" (1 Corinthians 15:45,47). Where the first Adam failed, the second Adam would succeed. Why? Because the second Adam would be divine: Jesus Christ.

Yet Jesus wouldn't show up on the scene for quite some time, so the entire Old Testament speaks in anticipation of this coming King who would one day rule on earth from the perspective of heaven. He would come through the Jews, sit on the throne of David, and oversee and rule the world from Israel. The prophets anticipated this King. God's covenant with Abraham anticipated this King. David's royal lineage anticipated this King. Zechariah 9:9 gives us insight into the thoughts of those who looked for King Jesus:

> Rejoice greatly, O daughter of Zion! Shout in triumph, O daughter of Jerusalem! Behold, your king is coming to you; He is just and endowed with salvation, humble, and mounted on a donkey, even on a colt, the foal of a donkey.

We shouldn't be surprised that when Jesus was ready to

reveal His kingship, He told His disciples to get Him a donkey, since it had been prophesied that the divine King would ride on one. We shouldn't be shocked that the magi came to worship Him after His birth, claiming that He was born King of the Jews (Matthew 2:2). When John the Baptist announced the King's arrival, he phrased it in terms the nation of Israel could understand: "Repent, for the kingdom of heaven is at hand" (Matthew 3:2). And when Jesus began preaching, He stepped onto the stage of history and said the same thing. "From that time Jesus began to preach and say, 'Repent, for the kingdom of heaven is at hand'" (Matthew 4:17). Furthermore, as He sent His disciples to preach, He told them to proclaim the kingdom of God had arrived (Matthew 10:7).

The King had come. His name was Jesus.

Submitting to the King's Rule

When we speak of Jesus, one of the names we aren't so quick to call Him by in today's culture—although it was hugely attributed to Him throughout all Scripture—is King. We recognize Him as Savior. We see that He is the living Lamb. We sing about Him as Immanuel. We tend to portray or visualize Jesus primarily in redemptive roles. And while these roles are key, I am afraid that in focusing so heavily on them, we miss out on much of Jesus' power in our daily lives. This power shows up in the names we get to know and align ourselves under, such as King, Lord, and Great High Priest.

Sure, redemption appeals to us in our autonomous, me-centric culture. We tend to be highly independent and self-serving, and many would even argue that our culture has given rise to an epidemic of narcissistic thinking. To acknowledge Jesus as King conjures up responses of obedience, dependence, honor, respect, and self-sacrifice. It goes against what our culture tells us is the way to live our lives.

Regardless, Jesus is King, and I've chosen to discuss this name near the start of the book because its importance is far reaching. Unless and until we understand and submit to Christ's rightful rule, we will not fully experience His power. Much of the chaos and challenges we cannot overcome in our lives stem from the fact that we do not rightly respond to His rule. If we make our own rules while living in the domain of a ruling King, then we should expect to face the consequences.

We understand that there are consequences when we break the laws of our nation or employer. For example, we can't simply make up our own rules regarding red lights and green lights or paying taxes—or when we are to report to work. And yet we rarely make the connection between personal disaster and mounting issues in our life as a result of living according to our own rules, not those of our King. If Jesus wrote us a ticket each time we disobeyed His commands on love, humility, giving to others, moral purity, and honoring Him first, maybe then we would more easily understand the cause and effect when it comes to breaking His rules. But He doesn't. And so we don't. And then we wind up asking Him to bail us out of what He Himself has sanctioned for us as a result of our sinful choices.

Jesus is King. Yet, like the Israelites of His day, we often praise Him one moment, only to seek to crucify Him the next. Why? Because we don't mind Him being King by name as long as He is not King by authority. We don't mind Jesus carrying around the title as long as He's not telling us what to do.

Friend, let me explain something about God's kingdom: It's not a democracy. He's not asking for your vote. He's not seeking your permission. God is a monarch. He declares what gets done, how things run, and what the goals of His kingdom will be.

As a parent, have you ever told your kids what you want them to do only to have them start a debate about it? You tell them what you want, and then they give you their unrequested opinion. Not only that, but then they argue with you about why your opinion is wrong—even though they are living in your house, under your roof, and under your authority. We do the same with God more often then we probably want to admit. To say that Jesus is King and declare that He is the ruler of His kingdom and yet argue His truth, disobey His commands, and spurn His rebukes is outright rebellion. As King, Jesus has the final say-so on every single subject. As His disciples, we are not only to preach His kingdom (Matthew 24:14), but we are also to live it out in our own lives.

Understanding Your Role in the Kingdom

Our role as Jesus' disciples involves more than sharing with others how they can obtain salvation. Our role involves modeling and telling others how to get heaven's rule down to earth. When someone trusts Jesus as their personal Savior, that gets them into the sweet by-and-by. And when that same someone discovers the importance of living their life under His kingdom rule, they uncover the power of having His rule join them in the nasty here and now.

Unfortunately, we often focus far more on how to get people to heaven, and so they wind up living broken, unempowered, and desperate lives on earth. Unless and until a follower of Jesus aligns himself under His rule, that follower will not experience the full benefits of His kingdom or His authority in their life. Jesus is King, and He demands allegiance in His kingdom. Yes, Jesus longs to be our Savior, but He also wants to be our ruler. He wants to be the one who has the final say over all matters in our life.

See, a kingdom is a domain over which a ruler sits and exercises authority. The kingdom of heaven refers to the jurisdiction over which God rules through Christ. When Jesus said that His kingdom is "not of this world" (John 18:36), He did not mean that His kingdom is not in this world. Rather, He meant that His kingdom authority does not originate from this world. The authority He exercises in this world comes from the world He came from—the heavenly realm—and He makes it clear that He is the King of this kingdom (John 18:37). That is why when we pray, we are to ask for God's will in heaven to be carried out on earth (Matthew 6:10). We are the mechanism through whom God's rule from above gets commissioned and effectuated on earth.

As Jesus' disciples, we are to sit under His rule and use it to govern and manage the spheres of influence He's bestowed on us here on earth. The problem is that many of us don't mind ascribing rule and authority to Jesus when we agree with Him. We just don't want to do that when we disagree. We want Jesus to have the final say over the decisions we like or the rules that make us feel comfortable. But that's not how kings rule. The concept of rulership is not that the king adjusts to the subject. No, the subject must adjust to the king.

Problems arise when we don't even bother to get to know Jesus and His Word in such a way that He can speak into every area of our lives. If you broke a speed limit because you didn't know it was the speed limit, do you think the judge would take that as a good excuse? Even if you told the judge that you didn't know better, you didn't see the sign, or you felt the limit was too slow for that area, the judge is still going to make you pay.

It's our role to understand the rules. God has given us everything we need to live according to His authority (see 2 Timothy 3:14-17). His revealed will provides the boundaries and parameters for us to make choices aligned under Him. His living Word and the Holy Spirit illuminate His truth in our minds in such a way as to provide direction and guidance as well. We have no excuse when we disobey God. Far too many Benedict Arnolds exist in His kingdom, working for the other side, all the while seeking the benefits He brings their way. But it doesn't work that way. To receive the benefits of the king-dom, you need to obey the King.

This is no small issue. God instructs us to make heavenly decisions in our earthly movements and direction. We are to live all of life under the kingdom agenda. You and I don't get to decide what defines gender. We don't get to decide what defines the institution of marriage. We don't get to decide if pride, obsession with social media, or narcissism are right ways to live. We don't get to decide the framework within which we are to manage our finances. We don't get to decide whether or not slacking off at work is acceptable. We don't get to decide if lusting after someone is okay—whether in person or online. We don't get to decide if racism, sexism, and classism are fine for us. These things, and everything else, have already been decided for us. God has spoken, and He has not stuttered.

Yet far too many people come into God's kingdom with their old way of thinking and their old rules. They enter His kingdom holding allegiance to their former ruler, the flesh. Relying on how you were raised, what your friends say, what your flesh desires, or what the media and culture purports as positive is only going to stir up conflict with your new ruler, Christ the King. Just like you would experience conflict if your teenage kids were to bring their friends into your home and they all chose to abide by their rules and not yours.

When I used to argue with my dad as a teenager, he had a response he used to say frequently: "Son, you haven't lived here long enough to know how to call the shots." When it comes to the King of kings and the Lord of lords who is from everlasting to everlasting, what He says stands. We haven't lived here long enough to know how to call all the shots. Our decisions must align under His decisions, or our decisions are wrong.

Some time ago when I visited New York with my wife, we stopped along the street where a large crowd had gathered. The crowd was waving their hands around at the display window, so we moved in closer to see what was going on. Apparently, Macy's had decided to use live models as mannequins in this display, and everyone passing by was trying to get them to budge. Yet, despite all the distractions, the models didn't move. Why? Because the people outside the windows weren't the ones paying them. The owners of Macy's were paying them, and so their obligation was to the owners, not to the crowd.

When you accept Jesus Christ as your Savior, you also accept an obligation to honor Him as your King. You are to follow what He says, not what the crowd says. You are not to be committed to this world order. It doesn't matter how many people like or dislike your decisions or how many people argue with you or put you down—none of that matters. The only question that matters is, "What does the King say?" Because He rules. He is your authority.

Matthew 6:33 tells us to seek first God's kingdom and His righteousness, and everything else will fall in line. In other words, when you seek the King's rule and honor first, He's got your back. If you want to seek your own will and kingdom, then you're going to need to have your own back as well. You don't get it both ways.

I like the way Luke phrases it in Luke 12:31-32. He says, "Seek His kingdom, and these things will be added to you. Do not be afraid, little flock, for your Father has chosen gladly to give you the kingdom." In other words, God is happy, thrilled, and will gladly give you the kingdom when you put Him first. It's His pleasure to do so.

A lot of us are missing out on the things that God wants to do in our hearts, relationships, finances, jobs, and cir-cumstances simply because we refuse to put God first in our thoughts, attitudes, and decisions. One of the reasons so many people remain defeated for so long is that they do not treat Jesus as King. It's true that the flesh will always seek to nullify

Jesus' authority. It pushes back against His commands. But one way to overcome the flesh is to give Jesus permission to tell you what to do. Then obey Him. Let Jesus tell you what to do about alcohol, pornography, your tongue, heart, relationships, hope, and faith. Let His rule overrule your flesh, and you will be set free.

Entering into the kingdom doesn't only mean getting into heaven. Far too many believers are satisfied with entering in the door (John 10:9), and they wind up staying stuck there. While salvation is essential and freedom from judgment is enormous, these are not the end of the story. Jesus saved you so that you could inherit His kingdom, a whole new realm of divine rule under His kingship. It is under His rule that you must let go of or adjust your history, background, secular education and thinking, cultural influence, pain, and regrets while looking to Him to guide you. Yes, there will be a clash as your flesh wars against the spirit and the spirit wars against the flesh. Sadly, a lot of people get confused about what they should do when the clash occurs.

Many assume if they just get closer to Jesus, the war between the flesh and the spirit will go away. And while getting relationally closer to Jesus is absolutely critical, obeying Him is just as critical—if not more so. In fact, obedience is a key component of increasing intimacy with our King (John 15:10-11). Recognizing Him as King is what will get your flesh to succumb to the rule of the spirt. Until you establish who is truly in charge, you will wind up making all sorts of excuses not to deal with the reality of Jesus' authority. Yes, Jesus loves you. Yes,

Jesus comforts you. Yes, Jesus provides for you. But Jesus also rules over you. And when you choose to disobey Him, you choose to remove yourself from His kingdom benefits.

Citizens of Heaven

Too many people want a savior, but they don't want a king. They don't want Jesus Christ to call the shots or have the final say. As a result, conflict upon conflict upon conflict all erupts into a giant mess. Philippians 3:20 tells us, "Our citizenship is in heaven, from which also we eagerly wait for a Savior, the Lord Jesus Christ." You and I are first and foremost citizens of heaven. Bear in mind that citizenship refers to your official place of residency. We are residents of the kingdom, and because we belong to the kingdom, we abide by its covenants and rules. Our King has conferred to us a kingdom (Luke 22:28-30).

If you travel abroad, then you have a passport. That passport allows you to leave the realm of your national citizenship and enter into another nation. It allows you to visit other countries or kingdoms. The passport identifies you and defines you with regard to your citizenship, so much so that the governing rules of your home nation will apply to you within your nation's embassy—no matter what country you are in.

Similarly, as a citizen of heaven, Jesus does not expect you to leave your passport at home. When you go to work, hang out with friends, or post online, Jesus does not want you to pretend to be someone else. You are part of the kingdom of heaven and ought to represent the kingdom in a way that brings it honor.

See, what a lot of Christians want is to live here on earth without a heavenly passport. They'd prefer dual citizenship. But it doesn't work that way. Jesus Christ, as our King, has established the dictates under which we are to live. There will be consequences when we decide to go against Him. When we live outside Jesus' kingdom mandates, we lose access to His kingdom authority operating on our behalf.

Jesus' name is King. He is our ruler. He is the final authority, and He calls the shots. Matthew 28:18 says, "Jesus came up and spoke to them, saying, 'All authority has been given to Me in heaven and on earth.'" Not some. Not part. Not a tad. *All*.

True, this is a side of Jesus we don't talk about much. But since all authority belongs to Him, don't you think it would be wise to obey Him? He holds the authority to reverse whatever challenge you are facing. He holds the authority to overcome those coworkers who are seeking to bring you down at work. He holds the authority to turn your financial mess around, restore your marriage, or lead you in fulfilling your destiny. He's in charge—of everything. Even your trials. Even your issues. Even your enemies. What's more, He holds authority over the greatest enemy of all time, Satan himself. Revelation 17:14 says, "These will wage war against the Lamb, and the Lamb will overcome them, because He is Lord of lords and King of kings, and those who are with Him are the called and chosen and faithful." And then in Revelation 19 we read:

> On His robe and on His thigh He has a name written, "KING OF KINGS, AND LORD OF LORDS"… And I saw the beast and the kings of

the earth and their armies assembled to make war against Him who sat on the horse and against His army… And the rest were killed with the sword which came from the mouth of Him who sat on the horse (verses 16,19,21).

In this final war, Jesus is going to show those who think they have power that He is the King of all kings. Jesus is over all. That's why you don't have to live an intimidated life anymore. It doesn't matter if someone has a position that is higher than yours, more money than you, better looks than you, or seemingly more power than you. Anyone who has authority over you, Jesus has greater authority over them. It's only when we seek to overcome our own battles in our own ways and with our own wisdom that we lose.

Look to Jesus' rule, abide by His covenant, and live under His authority with His righteousness, and He will overcome whatever you face that goes against Him. No human being has the last word over you, because no human being is the King of kings. They may be *a* king, but they are not *the* King. They may be *a* boss, but they are not *the* boss. They may be *an* authority, but they are not *the* authority. Jesus isn't only the nice, meek babe in the manger we know Him to be. He's powerful, authoritative, and will win any war you turn over to Him. He's your general, chief, warrior, combatant, and most importantly, your King.

The blood shall be a sign for you on the houses where you live; and when I see the blood I will pass over you, and no plague will befall you to destroy you when I strike the land of Egypt.

EXODUS 12:13

The next day he saw Jesus coming to him and said, "Behold, the Lamb of God who takes away the sin of the world!"

JOHN 1:29

4

LAMB OF GOD

How can a king also be a lamb? Don't those two roles seem to contradict each other? Isn't a lamb meek and mild? After all, it is a helpless animal lacking much in insight and smarts. It can be difficult to envision how Jesus can embody the qualities of both a lamb and a king. But once you get to the know the Lamb of God as He is to be fully known in Scripture, you will come to see that the Lamb is actually a fierce and mighty King. In fact, the Lamb is the name to which you should appeal when you wage your most challenging wars. The Lamb is worthy of your greatest honor, fear, and respect.

But let's not get too far ahead of ourselves. Let's start where the role of a lamb originated and see how Jesus fulfills it before looking more closely at the warrior Lamb who will one day rule. Unfortunately, far too many people want to skip the beginning and the importance of the sacrificial Lamb, and that is why they never come to discover the power of the Lamb in their everyday lives.

When Adam and Eve first sinned in the garden, they tried to fix the problem themselves. Sewing some fig leaves together, they then tied those leaves around their bodies to try to cover their shame. But God did not accept that covering. The sewing of fig leaves did not satisfy the demands of a holy God. As a result, God had to slay an animal Himself and shed blood in order to provide a covering for Adam and Eve that He would accept (see Genesis 3:7,21). This one act then led to an entire sacrificial system that took place throughout the Old Testament by which the wrath of God could be temporarily assuaged.

The main centerpiece of this program, an event called the Passover, can be found in Exodus 12. When the people of Israel were preparing to leave their bondage of slavery in Egypt, the last plague God performed involved taking the lives of the firstborn in the land. In order for the Israelites to bypass what God had said He would do, they were instructed to take the blood of an unblemished lamb and paint it on the doorposts of their home. When the Lord came by their home, He would recognize the sacrifice and pass over that home, leaving everyone inside it still alive. We read about this in Exodus 12:13.

> The blood shall be a sign for you on the houses where you live; and when I see the blood I will pass over you, and no plague will befall you to destroy you when I strike the land of Egypt.

In other words, the blood would avert judgment based on God's justice. The reason why it had to be blood on the doorposts rather than anything else is because of this principle found in Scripture: "The life of the flesh is in the blood" (Leviticus 17:11). If a person loses too much blood, they lose their life. And God says there must be the shedding of blood in order to avert His wrath.

A Sufficient Sacrifice

God is holy. God is just. He is not merely reactional when it comes to His response to sin. He doesn't just lose it and get mad. Rather, God's wrath is tied to His justice, and His justice is part of His nature. And while God doesn't prefer wrath, He can't skip justice. He has to exercise it. Thus, out of His great mercy and grace, He came up with a way to avert His wrath.

This temporary solution in the Old Testament involved the slaying of the lamb as well as other prescribed sacrifices. When God saw the blood, He accepted it in what we might compare to a "layaway plan." Animal sacrifices never provided full payment for the problem of sin, although they delayed the full punishment. The reason they never provided full payment was because they were not equal sacrifices. In other words, man was the sinner, but the lamb was the sacrifice. The sacrificed being had to be equal to the nature of the one for whom the sacrifice was for in order for it to accomplish the full payment (Hebrews 10:4).

The sacrifice needed to be spotless, sinless. It had to be perfect, without disease. It couldn't have anything wrong with it. And even though a lamb is sinless, it could not sin by nature of its existence, so the sacrifice was not in line with what it needed to cover. Hebrews 10:11-14 provides the greatest contrast between the sacrifices of the past and the one who fulfilled all.

> Every priest stands daily ministering and offer-
> ing time after time the same sacrifices, which can
> never take away sins; but He, having offered one
> sacrifice for sins for all time, sat down at the right
> hand of God, waiting from that time onward
> until His enemies be made a footstool for His feet.
> For by one offering He has perfected for all time
> those who are sanctified.

The old system provided a delay, but it was a system that required repetition. Every year, the high priest had to go into the Holy of Holies to present the sacrifice on the Day of Atonement. On top of that, all the people would need to offer their own sacrifices on a regular basis in order for God's judgment to bypass them. The sacrifice of a lamb was for the purpose of substitutionary atonement. Unless we first grasp the importance of this reality, we won't fully comprehend this name of Jesus. The bottom line is that God must judge sin. And we are sinful. Therefore, we are all under judgment.

Now, we don't all sin to the same degree, and we don't all sin in the same way, but when you are dealing with the categories of holiness and perfection, it doesn't matter whether you are a big sinner, medium sinner, or a tiny sinner. Any sin taints holiness just as any amount of arsenic would taint a pot of stew. The whole pot would need to be tossed once arsenic is introduced into the equation.

Some people think that because they keep most of the Ten Commandments they should be okay. But imagine you were hanging by a chain with ten links on it over the side of a cliff. If only one link breaks, what happens to you? Similarly, if you break only one of the Ten Commandments, you are no longer holy. God's standard is perfection, not merely being "pretty good." God only accepts what He accepts. He doesn't accept what you want Him to accept just because it's acceptable to you. Have you ever had someone do some work for you on your house, and they thought they did a good job, but you had to tell them you weren't satisfied with what they did? The reason why your viewpoint matters is because you are the owner of the house. Similarly, God's standard is what matters when it comes to His creation. He will accept nothing less than perfection. This is why it's important that Jesus is called the Lamb without spot or blemish (1 Peter 1:18-19; Hebrews 9:11-14). As the Lamb of God, Jesus fulfills this perfection.

First Corinthians 5:7 refers to Him as "our Passover lamb" (ESV). John 1:29 tells us, "The next day [John the Baptist] saw Jesus coming to him and said, 'Behold, the Lamb of God who takes away the sin of the world!'" If you read over those verses too quickly, you might miss something. You might miss one key phrase. This prepositional phrase is "of the world." When Jesus came as the Lamb of God, He provided a sacrifice known as *unlimited atonement*. The death of Jesus was so sufficient that it addressed every sin of every person who has ever lived—and will ever live—in all time. His sacrifice satisfies the demands for the whole world (1 John 2:2).

In 2 Corinthians 5:19 we read, "God was in Christ reconciling the world to Himself, not counting their trespasses against them, and He has committed to us the word of reconciliation." Through Jesus, God reconciled the entire world to Himself. Jesus is the Lamb of God who satisfied the demands of God because He met the standards of God. One of these standards was perfection. Jesus was perfect. Another standard was that the sacrifice had to be human. Jesus qualified. A third standard was that the sacrifice had to be like us. Hebrews 2:17 tells us, "He had to be made like His brethren in all things, so that He might become a merciful and faithful high priest in things pertaining to God, to make propitiation for the sins of the people."

Jesus had to have blood, skin, and bones. He had to understand struggle, pain, and loss. Jesus qualified for all that, and He was also perfect.

On the cross, Jesus Christ bore every sin of every person who has ever lived—for all time.

A very common misconception about heaven and hell is that people don't go to heaven—and subsequently do go to hell—because of their sins. If that were true, then even saved people couldn't go to heaven because saved people have still sinned. No, people don't go to hell because of their sins. Why? Because Jesus paid the sacrifice for *all* sins. His last words on the cross were, "It is finished!" (John 19:30). That means the penalty for sin has been paid in full.

The problem is that even though everyone's sins have been paid for, those who go to hell do not possess eternal life. John 3:16 tells us, "God so loved the world, that He gave His only begotten Son, that whoever believes in Him shall not perish, but have eternal life." What is missing is *life*. They have not chosen to receive the life that has been given to them. In fact, they have rejected it.

Let me try to illustrate this in a contemporary example. If I were to buy you a brand-new car and give it to you, the entire car would be paid for, even the taxes. The only catch would be that the car would still be at the dealership waiting for you to receive it. Now, if you chose not to go pick up the car, it would do you no good at all. Worse yet, if you chose to pick it up and drive it but still sent in monthly payments, you would be indicating that you do not believe the car is truly yours already.

Or what about birthday gifts? We get them every year. Have you ever been given a birthday gift and then proceeded to pay the person who gave it to you? Or has anyone ever done that to you? It's doubtful. Why? Because a gift is just that: a gift. Similarly, the gift of eternal life is not something we can earn, make payments on, or pay back. But we do have to receive it by placing our faith in Christ alone for the atonement of our sins. It is entirely possible for someone to have their sins paid for and yet not benefit from that payment because they choose not to believe.

People don't go to hell because they have sinned. Sin has been paid for. The reason they do not go to heaven—and thus, wind up in hell—is because they have not responded in faith to the one who paid for them to receive the gift of eternal life (Revelation 20:11-15). See, that's why the gospel is "good news." You don't have to pay for any of it. The great news of the gospel is that our sin debt has been paid in full. God allowed a permanent sacrifice—the Lamb of God—to substitute for the punishment each of us deserves. Second Corinthians 5:21 tells it this way: "He made Him who knew no sin to be sin on our behalf, so that we might become the righteousness of God in Him." God initiated a credit transfer. He took Jesus' righteousness and transferred His perfect "credit score" to each person who receives Christ through faith in Him.

So, even though you may have a terrible credit score on your own merit, when God looks at you, it is as though you have never sinned. You are acceptable to a perfect God because He has provided you with the righteousness of Jesus Christ. It's good news when you have a bill you do not have to pay—especially one you could never afford to pay.

The Theology of the Lamb

To understand the theology of the Lamb, we must first look at the theology of salvation itself. Now, if you are already saved, you may be tempted to skip over this section. But this portion of the chapter is written with two purposes in mind. First, for those who have never been acquainted with the basic foundations of the Christian faith, I want to present them clearly. Second, for those who have already become Christians, I want to teach a plain and powerful way to share their faith with others.

The Problem

"All have sinned and fall short of the glory of God" (Romans 3:23).

Salvation is good news, but it comes to us against a backdrop of bad news. The bad news is that we are all sinners. Not one man or woman on planet Earth—past, present, or future—is without sin.

The Greek word for *sin* literally means "to miss the mark." It describes a bowman who drew back his string, released his arrow, but failed to hit the bull's-eye. Similarly, sin involves missing the target. What is the target? Romans 3:23 tells us: "All have sinned and *fall short of the glory of God*" (emphasis added). Sin is falling short of God's glory—His standard.

To help you understand this concept, I must attack a popular myth maintained by the media, the literary community, and sometimes even the church itself. The fable is that sin can be measured by degree. To many of us, criminals seem like big-time sinners, while those of us who tell little white lies are lightweight sinners. It appears logical to believe that those in county jail have not sinned as seriously as those in the state penitentiary. But sin looks quite different from God's perspective.

In Scripture, sin is not measured by degree. Either we fall short of God's glory or we don't. Since the entire sin question pivots on this point, let's make sure we understand our target.

The word *glory* refers to something put on display—shown off. Sin is missing the mark, and the mark is to properly "put God on display." When we view the issue from this perspective, our understanding of sin begins to change. Any time we ever do anything that does not accurately reveal who and what God is, any time we fail to reflect the character of God, then we have sinned.

The story is told of two men who were exploring an island when, suddenly, a volcano erupted. In moments, the two found themselves surrounded by molten lava. Several feet away was a clearing—and a path to safety. To get there, however, they would have to jump across the river of melted rock. The first man was an active senior citizen but hardly an outstanding physical specimen. He ran as fast as he could, took an admirable leap, but traveled only a few feet. He met a swift death in the superheated lava.

The other explorer was a much younger, more virile man in excellent physical condition. In fact, the college record he set in the broad jump had remained unbroken to that day. He put all his energy into his run, jumped with flawless form, and shattered his own college record. Unfortunately, he landed far short of the clearing. Though the younger man clearly outper- formed his companion, both wound up equally dead. Survival was so far out of reach that their ability became a non-issue.

Degrees of "goodness" may be important when hiring an employee or choosing friends. But when the issue is sin, the only standard that matters is God's perfect holiness. The ques- tion is not how you measure up against the guy down the street, but how you measure up to God. God's standard is perfect righteousness, and it is a standard that even the best behaved or most morally upright person still cannot reach.

The Penalty

"Just as sin entered the world through one man, and death through sin, and in this way death came to all people, because all sinned" (Romans 5:12 NIV).

After reading this verse, you may be thinking, *If sin entered the world through one man (Adam), it isn't fair to punish the rest of us.* Yet death spread to all men "because all sinned." We are not punished simply because Adam sinned, but because we inherited Adam's propensity to sin and have sinned ourselves.

Have you ever noticed that you don't need to teach your children how to sin? Can you imagine sitting down with your child and saying, "Here's how to lie successfully," or "Let me show you how to be selfish"? Those things come naturally.

Let me illustrate this another way. Have you ever seen an apple with a small hole in it? If you have, you were most likely hesitant to eat the apple. The presence of the hole suggested there was a worm in there waiting for you. Now, most people don't know how the worm managed to take up residence in that apple. They think a full-grown worm was slithering by one day when he decided to bore through the outer skin of the fruit and set up house inside. However, that is not what happens. Worm larvae hatch from eggs dropped on the fruit or leaves. As young larvae, they make their home in the fruit. The hole is left when the grown worm later digs his way out.

Similarly, the seed of sin is within each and every one of us at the moment of birth. Though it may take some time before the evidence of sin shows on the surface, it is there and eventually makes its presence known.

Sin demands a penalty. That penalty, according to Scripture, is death (see Romans 6:23). That means both physical death (where the soul is separated from the body) and spiritual death (where the soul is separated from God).

The Provision

"But God demonstrates his own love for us in this: While we were still sinners, Christ died for us" (Romans 5:8 NIV).

"But God" are two very powerful words. They can revolutionize any situation. *My marriage is falling apart. But God... My husband abandoned us, and my children are out of control. But God... I have no job, no income, and no future. But God...*

God can restore any situation. He is bigger and more powerful than any life challenge or predicament or result from sin.

I'm a sinner condemned to eternal separation from God. But God... Those words sum up the theology of salvation for each of us. Even while we were still sinners, God proved His love for us by sending Jesus Christ, His righteous Lamb, to die in our place.

How amazing that God would love us so deeply. We have certainly done nothing to deserve it. But the amazement intensifies when you consider the significance of Jesus' sacrifice on Calvary.

Not just anybody could die for the penalty of sin. You see, we all have sinned, so none of us could die to pay that penalty. We each have our own price to pay. Whoever would save us must be perfectly sinless.

Consider this illustration. Two brothers were playing in the woods one summer day when, almost without warning, a bee flew down and stung the older brother on the eyelid. He put his hands to his face and fell to the ground in pain. As the younger brother looked on in horror, the bee began buzzing around his head. Terrified, he began screaming, "The bee's going to get me!" The older brother, regaining his composure, said, "What are you talking about? That bee can't hurt you. He's already stung me."

The Bible tells us that this is what happened on Calvary. God loves you so much that He stepped out of heaven in the person of Jesus Christ and took the "stinger of death" in your place. Jesus hung on the cross, not for His own sin, but for yours and mine. Because Jesus Christ is without sin, His death paid the penalty for all of us (2 Corinthians 5:21).

How do we know that Jesus' death on the cross really took care of the sin problem? Because of what happened that Sunday. When Mary Magdalene came to Jesus' tomb that morning, she couldn't find Him. She saw someone and thought it was a gardener. She asked Him where the Lord's body had been taken. When the gardener said her name, Mary gasped in amazement. It was Jesus (see John 20:1-18).

According to 1 Corinthians 15:6, more than 500 people personally saw the risen Christ before He ascended into heaven. If not for the resurrection, our faith would be empty and useless. As the apostle Paul said, if Jesus were not raised, we should be the most pitied people on earth. But the fact is, the Lamb of God *has* been raised (1 Corinthians 15:12-20).

The Pardon

"To the one who works, his wage is not credited as a favor, but as what is due. But to the one who does not work, but believes in Him who justifies the ungodly, his faith is credited as righteousness" (Romans 4:4-5). "For by grace you have been saved through faith; and that not of yourselves, it is the gift of God; not as a result of works, so that no one may boast" (Ephesians 2:8-9).

If good works could save anyone, there would have been no point in Jesus' death. But Jesus knew we couldn't pay sin's price. That's why His sacrifice as the Lamb of God was vital. In order for His sacrifice to secure our pardon, we must trust in Him for our salvation.

Believing *in* Jesus means a great deal more than believing *about* Jesus. Knowing the facts about His life and death is mere "head knowledge." Believing in Jesus demands that we put that knowledge to work. It means to trust in Him, to have total confidence in Him, to rest your case on Him. Without realizing it, you illustrate this concept every time you sit down. The moment you commit your weight to a chair, you have "believed in" that chair to hold you up. Most of us have so much faith in chairs that, despite our weight, we will readily place ourselves down without a second thought.

If a tinge of doubt creeps in, you might steady yourself by grabbing something with your hand or by keeping your legs beneath you, resting only part of your weight on the chair. That's what many people do with salvation. They're reasonably sure that Jesus is who He says He is. However, they hedge their bet by putting some of their trust in their efforts at good behavior, their church traditions, or anything else they can do.

You must understand that if you depend on anything beyond Jesus for your salvation, then what you're really saying is that Jesus Christ is not enough.

God is waiting for you to commit the entire weight of your existence to Jesus Christ and what He did on the cross. Your complete eternal destiny must rest upon Him.

You might say, "But my mom was a Christian, and she prayed for me." Praise God. But what about you? Christianity has nothing to do with your heritage. It has nothing to do with the name of the church you attend. It has to do with whether you have placed absolute confidence in the person and work of Christ alone.

The Lamb of God provides the redemption for our sins. Romans 3:24 tells us, "Being justified as a gift by His grace through the redemption which is in Christ Jesus." If you remember S & H Green Stamps, then this verse will make all the more sense to you. A person could redeem Green Stamps they received from other stores when they purchased something. They would be able to trade in those stamps for something at the redemption center. This is exactly what redemption means—to release the payment or price of an item. Back when slavery was legal in America, slaves would sometimes be "redeemed" when someone would pay the price placed on them and then set them free. The Lamb of God paid the price we owe in order to redeem us from our sins.

In addition to providing justification and redemption, Jesus also served as the propitiation for our sins. We see this in Romans 3:25, which says, "God displayed [Jesus] publicly as a propitiation in His blood through faith. This was to demonstrate His righteousness, because in the forbearance of God He passed over the sins previously committed." *Propitiation* is a big theological term that means "satisfaction." To be propitiated means to be satisfied. Thus, when we say that the Lamb of God satisfied the demands of a holy God with His substitutionary atonement, we are declaring that He is the propitiation for our sins.

The Lamb of God offers eternal life to all who respond to His gift of justification, redemption, and propitiation. First John 2:2 tells us that He was not only the propitiation for our sins, but also for the sins of the whole world. If we reject the grace of the Lamb, then we must endure the wrath of the

Lamb (Revelation 6:15-17). First Peter 2:24 emphasizes this: "He Himself bore our sins in His body on the cross, so that we might die to sin and live to righteousness; for by His wounds you were healed."

Our response to the Lamb of God should be to live righteously. He died so that you and I could live in spiritual victory, not spiritual defeat. He died so the devil would no longer own us. In this way, His death not only saves us for heaven, but it also saves us and rescues us on earth. By His stripes, we are healed in our daily life. We are healed from addictions, fear, worry, relational issues, doubt, and much more.

Perhaps you have not yet experienced this healing. You may still struggle with wounds from pain or sin in the past. But what the Lamb of God secured is a redemption so powerful that He can heal all the wounds you still have. See, Jesus' sacrifice on the cross was not made just so that sinners would become saints. It was also made so that saints would get healed. The Lamb of God didn't just save you for eternity; He saved you for right now.

No Ordinary Lamb

When you truly understand this name of Jesus and what He accomplished as the Lamb, it should affect how you live out your life. That's why I love Revelation 12:11, where it says, "They overcame [the accuser] because of the blood of the Lamb and because of the word of their testimony, and they did not love their life even when faced with death." Notice what this verse doesn't say. It doesn't say they overcame by the power of positive thinking. They didn't overcome by their own physical strength. They didn't overcome by how much money they had.

Scripture says they overcame by the blood of the Lamb. This is because on the cross, Jesus not only paid for your sins, but He also broke the authority of Satan. Too many times we hear sermons about Good Friday, sing songs about Friday, or think about His death on Friday. And all of that is good; it's just that we often forget about what happened on Saturday. On Saturday, Jesus went to hell and declared victory to the demonic realm (1 Peter 3:18-20; Ephesians 4:9).

Between His death and resurrection, the Lamb of God preached a victory sermon. He told the devil, "I win, and you lose! I am in charge." The debt owed to the devil was broken. It's over. So the only way the devil can own you now is to trick you. That's why he's called the great deceiver, because he now has to trick you into thinking that you don't have enough power. And the main way he does that is by getting you to forget about the blood of the Lamb. Because if you ever forget about the power of the blood, you will lose sight of what brings you overcoming victory in your life. The blood of the Lamb is what breaks the devil's back. It is the blood that gives you the power of righteousness.

When you wake up each morning, before your feet even hit the floor, you should declare to yourself and the devil the truth that the Lamb of God has dealt with all your sin. Not only enough to get you to heaven, but also enough to keep Satan off your back on earth.

This truth of this name of Jesus is so important that it ought to be a regular part of your thought process and day. It ought to be what you go to first when life's troubles come your way. Appeal to the blood of the Lamb when you face issues of any kind, because the root of all spiritual warfare is spiritual in nature.

More than 20 times in the book of Revelation, Jesus is called by this name. This final book of Scripture, which holds the mystery of God's coming kingdom, references Jesus as the Lamb over and over and over again. The slain Lamb is the only one who is able to open the book of judgment.

- *Revelation 5:6*—"I saw between the throne (with the four living creatures) and the elders a Lamb standing, as if slain, having seven horns and seven eyes, which are the seven Spirits of God, sent out into all the earth."

- *Revelation 5:8*—"When He had taken the book, the four living creatures and the twenty-four elders fell down before the Lamb, each one holding a harp and golden bowls full of incense, which are the prayers of the saints."

- *Revelation 6:1*—"I saw when the Lamb broke one of the seven seals, and I heard one of the four living creatures saying as with a voice of thunder, 'Come.'"

- *Revelation 7:9*—"I looked, and behold, a great multitude which no one could count, from every nation and all tribes and peoples and tongues, standing before the throne and before the Lamb, clothed in white robes, and palm branches were in their hands."

- *Revelation 17:14*—"These [kings] will wage war

against the Lamb, and the Lamb will overcome
them, because He is Lord of lords and King of
kings, and those who are with Him are the called
and chosen and faithful."

Time and again John references the Lamb as ruler, the one
we will worship, our warrior and redeemer. He's a lion who
brings wrath (Revelation 5:5). And in verses 11-14, we see the
greatest overall description of the Lamb of God:

> I looked, and I heard the voice of many angels
> around the throne and the living creatures and
> the elders; and the number of them was myriads
> of myriads, and thousands of thousands, saying
> with a loud voice, "Worthy is the Lamb that was
> slain to receive power and riches and wisdom and
> might and honor and glory and blessing." And
> every created thing which is in heaven and on the
> earth and under the earth and on the sea, and all
> things in them, I heard saying, "To Him who sits
> on the throne, and to the Lamb, be blessing and
> honor and glory and dominion forever and ever."
> And the four living creatures kept saying, "Amen."
> And the elders fell down and worshiped.

This is no ordinary lamb. This is the Lamb of God, who
takes away the sins of the world and is worthy of our worship.
He sits on the throne. He wages victorious warfare. He receives
power, might, and honor. This is the DNA of the Lamb of
God. We ought to make worshiping Him a lifestyle because,
in so doing, we activate the power He died to provide.

I recently filmed a Bible study in Jackson Hole, Wyoming.

It's a beautiful part of the country, full of some of our nation's finest examples of nature and wildlife. One thing I noticed as we traveled throughout the various parts of the sanctuary where we filmed is that there were frequent signs reminding people to carry bear spray. Now, bear spray is designed to be used in warding off oncoming wild bears. Just a few days after we flew out, a travel guide was attacked and killed by a bear. So they are no small danger, but bear spray can keep them safely at bay.

Similarly, the blood of the Lamb is our repellent for Satan. When Satan starts to mess with you in your home, on your job, or in your emotions and thoughts, you need to worship the Lamb of God. In doing so, you are overcoming Satan with the all-powerful blood. It is the blood of the Lamb that will gain you victory—not only for eternity, but also for every single moment of your life. But you activate the power of the blood through your worship of Him and alignment under Him.

Satan is no mild enemy. He has claws. He has strength. His jaws can crush you. He is deceptive and comes at you through a variety of attempts to take you off track from living out your kingdom destiny for God. It is only when you activate the power of Jesus' blood as your covering and as your spiritual weaponry that you will walk in victory.

Understand this name. Worship this name. Apply this name. Honor this name. It is in this name that you will find protection, power, and strength. Worthy is the Lamb.

The Lord has sworn and will not change His mind,
"You are a priest forever according to the order of
Melchizedek."

PSALM 110:4

Therefore, since we have a great high priest who has
passed through the heavens, Jesus, the Son of God, let
us hold fast our confession...let us draw near with
confidence to the throne of grace, so that we may
receive mercy and find grace to help in time of need.

HEBREWS 4:14,16

5

GREAT HIGH PRIEST

So far we have come to know Jesus more deeply as Immanuel, the Alpha and Omega, our King, and the mighty Lamb. But linking these all together is another unique role that Jesus fulfills as He meets the unblemished perfection of God's high standards. We discover this role in His name of Great High Priest, found predominantly in one of the most misunderstood books of the Bible: Hebrews. Admittedly, Hebrews is one of the more difficult books of the Bible to comprehend. Most people consider it the second most difficult New Testament book to understand after Revelation. One of the reasons Hebrews can be so confusing is that the book was written with an assumption. That assumption is that its readers had a solid understanding of the Old Testament.

In the Old Testament, we see many sacrifices, symbols, regulations, and systems in place that contributed to the daily routine of people's lives. And while Jews living in the day that

Hebrews was written would have been entirely familiar with all of this and more, most of us living today simply are not.

Many of us don't come from that background. We are not steeped in Old Testament tradition or theology, the sacrificial system, nor the biblical priesthood. As a result, it is unclear to many of us what Hebrews is even talking about.

If I were to summarize the main point and message of the book of Hebrews for you, I would do it in three words: Never give up. That's the bottom line of all the peculiar elements of this book.

Never give up.

This book was written to a group of believers who were severely struggling with throwing in the towel. They were tempted to walk away from the faith. They were tempted to give up or give in because life had become too hard. Living as a Christian in their culture had become too difficult. They faced persecution, pressure, challenges, and overwhelming odds on a daily basis. Life was hard. Which is why the author of Hebrews sought to remind them not to quit. Not to give in. Not to give up. Not to let their hearts, which had already grown weary, simply stop.

You might be able to identify with the audience of Hebrews. You might find yourself in dire situations and feel tempted to quit. It could be you are raising the question, "Why go on?" You feel that things will never change. It simply isn't going to get any better. You may think you will never find the victory you are looking for or discover the life you hope to live.

Even though we are Christians, go to church, say our prayers, and seek the Lord, there are times when each of us (if we're honest) feel tempted to give up. There are times when we are merely holding on by a thread and feeling as if one small thing could tip us over.

But the author of the book of Hebrews seeks to explain why you don't have to give up or give in. And it all hinges on one name of Jesus: Great High Priest.

Qualifications of a Priest

To understand the significance of this name, you first need to understand the nature of the Judaic priesthood. The author of Hebrews gives us some insight at the beginning of chapter 5.

> Every high priest taken from among men is appointed on behalf of men in things pertaining to God, in order to offer both gifts and sacrifices for sins; he can deal gently with the ignorant and misguided, since he himself also is beset with weakness; and because of it he is obligated to offer sacrifices for sins, as for the people, so also for himself. And no one takes the honor to himself, but receives it when he is called by God, even as Aaron was (verses 1-4).

A priest had to be taken from men and appointed on behalf of men. In other words, a priest had to be equal to those whom he was serving in this role. The author of Hebrews goes on to say that the priest also had to be appointed by God. A person couldn't just wake up one morning and decide he wanted to be a priest. This was not a decision a person could make on his own. Neither could other people make someone a priest. They couldn't just write in a name on a ballot. There had to be a defining call by God.

In addition, the priest had to offer sacrifices for sins. He had to do this for his own sin, as well as for the sins of those he represented (verse 3). And while these sacrifices didn't remove the sin or its consequences, they did allow for a delay until the true sacrifice would one day come. We see this in Hebrews 10:4, which says, "It is impossible for the blood of bulls and goats to take away sins." These animal sacrifices reminded people that sin brings forth death. Since sin brings forth death, the animals would be killed to delay the judgment of death on those who had sinned.

There was another qualification that a priest had to have, which is revealed to us in Hebrews 5:2: "He can deal gently with the ignorant and misguided, since he himself also is beset with weakness." Essentially, the priest had to understand what it means to struggle. He had to be able to identify with those who experience issues in life. He couldn't be someone who did not know how to have compassion on those who need it the most. To have someone "beset with weakness" means that person has their own limitations and challenges as well.

If a person seeks to minister to others who has never experienced pain himself, he can come across as merely spouting information—and that information can often be shallow, unrealistic, and even idealistic. There is a learning curve that can only occur through personal trials and pain. A priest had to know this. He had to realize that he needed to be cleansed from his own sins and needed to seek divine help just like the people for whom he performed the sacrifices of atonement.

All these things give us a better concept of what it means for Jesus to be our Great High Priest. As it says in Hebrews 5:5-10...

So also Christ did not glorify Himself so as to
become a high priest, but He who said to Him,
"You are My Son, today I have begotten You";
just as He says also in another passage, "You are a
priest forever according to the order of Melchizedek." In the days of His flesh, He offered up both
prayers and supplications with loud crying and
tears to the One able to save Him from death,
and He was heard because of His piety. Although
He was a Son, He learned obedience from the
things which He suffered. And having been made
perfect, He became to all those who obey Him
the source of eternal salvation, being designated
by God as a high priest according to the order of
Melchizedek.

Notice that this passage begins with the phrase "so also."
This is a comparison reference. We are being told that Jesus
was everything that was just discussed in verses 1-4 regarding
the priesthood, plus everything about to be discussed as well.
He had to qualify just like the previous priests had to qualify.
He was appointed by God. He was human. He had to know
and understand suffering—to weep as we weep and to comprehend what it means to struggle. In His humanity, He identified with anguish, agony, pain, emptiness, and more. Just
like you and I do.

But even though Jesus qualified for the priesthood according to the rules established long ago, He filled one greater qualification that no one else had. We read about this in verses 6
and 10, where it says that Jesus came "according to the order
of Melchizedek." His lineage of priesthood was rooted in the

process, programming, and historical line of Melchizedek. In order to understand Jesus as a Great High Priest, then, we have to first understand Melchizedek.

Now, it's easy to tune out when someone brings up a name like Melchizedek. This happens for a number of reasons, one of which is simply that you might not even know how to pronounce the word. But even in the day and age that the book of Hebrews was written, people tuned out—despite a familiarity with Jewish culture and heritage. The author of this book tells us that the reason people tune out is because they have become "dull of hearing." We read this in Hebrews 5:11, which says, "Concerning him we have much to say, and it is hard to explain, since you have become dull of hearing."

This means that they, and many of us today, do not have spiritual ears. It means we are still thinking worldly, functioning worldly, and living by the flesh. It's like trying to listen to an FM station on an AM dial. It won't work unless you switch to FM. When we as Christians live a carnal existence, spiritual truths swoop right over our heads. We miss the point being made. But the problem is if we miss the point being made on Melchizedek, then we'll also miss the point being made about Jesus. Which means we will also miss the help we need to receive in order to face the problems and issues in front of us.

Meet Melchizedek

Melchizedek's name is only found twice in the entire Old Testament. We read about him in Psalm 110:4, where it says, "The Lord has sworn and will not change His mind, 'You are a priest forever according to the order of Melchizedek.'"

We also read about him in Genesis 14, where it says...

> After [Abram's] return from the defeat of Che-
> dorlaomer and the kings who were with him, the
> king of Sodom went out to meet him at the val-
> ley of Shaveh (that is, the King's Valley). And
> Melchizedek king of Salem brought out bread
> and wine; now he was a priest of God Most High.
> He blessed him and said, "Blessed be Abram of
> God Most High, possessor of heaven and earth;
> and blessed be God Most High, who has deliv-
> ered your enemies into your hand" (verses 17-20).

Bottom line: Melchizedek is a king. He is the king of Salem.
During Old Testament times, Salem was a name for Jerusalem, and it means "peace." Thus, the king of Salem is the king
of peace.

Every king has a kingdom, so we know that by nature of
his role, Melchizedek had a kingdom. He had a domain over
which he ruled. This was a place where his word was final. But
on top of being a king, Melchizedek was also a priest.

As we've seen, the job of a priest was to represent humanity
before God. The job of a prophet was to represent God before
humanity. A prophet brought the Word of God to men, but a
priest brought the sins of the people to God and offered up sacrifices on their behalf. We know that Jesus is a prophet because
He is called the Word of God (see John 1). We also know that
He is both a priest and a king—just like Melchizedek.

The scene that introduces us to Melchizedek (in Genesis
14) is a scene following a battle. Abram has just come in from
a war. He has been fighting. He's been giving all that he's got.
He's been doing everything he can in order to secure a victory.

Yet in the midst of his homecoming, he runs into the king-priest named Melchizedek, and this king-priest gives him both bread and wine. Why? Because Abram was tired. Even though he had made it through the battle, he was weary and needed to be restored. Essentially, Melchizedek refreshed him.

But notice, with the refreshment of bread and wine came a blessing. We see this reflected in the New Testament when we read in 1 Corinthians 10:16, "Is not the cup of blessing which we bless a sharing in the blood of Christ? Is not the bread which we break a sharing in the body of Christ?" Jesus came in the order of Melchizedek, and we experience both refreshment and blessing through communion today. It is what the priesthood offered under Melchizedek back then in another way. Communion is not just eating a wafer and drinking some juice. No, it's designed to help you overcome and be refreshed from yesterday's battles, as well as to help you get ready for tomorrow's battles. It's designed to give you a fresh blessing.

This blessing is tied to the two sides of a conflict. You see, what we often do is come out of one conflict and then go into another one without either being refreshed in the Lord or having the blessing activated on our behalf. That's why we wind up defeated on all sides. Jesus, your Great High Priest, has come to restore your spirit, give you strength, and provide you with a blessing in between the challenges and trials life brings.

Not only does Jesus bring us refreshment and blessing in His role as the Great High Priest, but He also brings us a stability for our soul and a unique level of intimacy with God. We see this as we read further in the book of Hebrews.

> This hope we have as an anchor of the soul, a hope both sure and steadfast and one which enters within the veil, where Jesus has entered as a forerunner for us, having become a high priest forever according to the order of Melchizedek (6:19-20).

Jesus is the anchor for the soul. What does an anchor do? It holds a boat steady. When the boat drops anchor, the anchor then keeps the boat in place despite how windy or stormy it might be. Even though the boat may be rocking, it never leaves its location because the anchor holds.

The reason you need to recognize this concept is because if you don't drop the anchor, it does you no good. If you don't allow Jesus as the Great High Priest to be present in your life as an anchor, then the storms of life will carry you away until you eventually crash. When you look to Him as the Great High Priest, letting Him steady you along the way because you are tied to Him firmly, then when things aren't working out at home, on the job, or with your finances, health, or your mental and emotional well-being, you will have an anchor. You will remain stable. In spite of the turbulence you face, Jesus will hold you steady. He will give you hope.

Hope is joyful expectation about the future. Hope is not concerned with where you are right now. Hope looks to where things are going to wind up. It always involves expectation. The high priesthood of Jesus Christ holds you steady while you wait with expectation. It keeps you grounded in the midst of the chaos you face.

Not only does Jesus bring refreshment, blessing, stability, and hope—He also gives us a greater intimacy with God by taking us behind the veil. See, the priest had to pass through three areas in the tabernacle. First, there was the outer court. Then he would walk into the Holy Place. After which he would walk into the Holy of Holies, where God's presence was. Jesus Christ, by virtue of His death, burial, and resurrection, has removed the veil that divides us from God the Father. We are now able to access the very presence of God because of our right relationship with Jesus, our Great High Priest.

An interesting thing about when the priest during the Old Testament times would enter into God's presence—it is said that they would have to tie a rope around his ankle. The rope was there in case the priest did something wrong in the presence of God. Maybe he touched something he shouldn't. Or maybe he had not gone through the purification process as he should have. Whatever the case, if he was struck dead, no one could go in and get him because no one else was authorized to enter into this holiest place. So if the priest died, they had to literally pull him out with a rope.

But Jesus has paid the price for our access. His righteousness has been imputed to us. We no longer need the rope because Jesus has made the pathway to the Father open to all who place their faith in Him. First John 2:2 tells us, "He Himself is the propitiation for our sins; and not for ours only, but also for those of the whole world." Jesus is our advocate with the Father (verse 1).

In Hebrews 7:1, we read that this role of priest after the order of Melchizedek includes serving as mediator: "This Melchizedek, king of Salem, priest of the Most High God, who met Abraham as he was returning from the slaughter of the kings and blessed him." Notice the reference to God here: Most High God. In the original language, this references God's name El Elyon. El Elyon is the name for God that means He rules over all. He is akin to the supreme court. No matter what a lower court says, the supreme court has the final say-so. Likewise, if God says differently than anyone else, then His rule is carried out as law. As our mediator and lawyer, Jesus serves us before the highest rule in the land.

Responding to the Great High Priest

What was Abram's response to Melchizedek—and what can we learn from it? He gave Melchizedek a gift, known as the tithe (see Genesis 14:20 and Hebrews 7:2). Now, many people don't want to hear about the tithe. They want to skip that part. But it's critical to understand because it's part of our relationship to the Great High Priest. In order to grasp the concept more fully, we need to look at some of the verses found in Hebrews 8.

- "The main point in what has been said is this: we have such a high priest, who has taken His seat at the right hand of the throne of the Majesty in the heavens" (verse 1).

- "If that first covenant had been faultless, there would have been no occasion sought for a second" (verse 7).

- "When He said, 'A new covenant,' He has made the first obsolete. But whatever is becoming obsolete and growing old is ready to disappear" (verse 13).

Many Christians today are operating under the wrong program when it comes to the tithe because they are operating under the Old Covenant concept of what a tithe contains. With the Old Covenant, a person had to give a tithe to get a blessing (see Malachi 3:10). That's not how things work under the New Covenant. Remember, it was Melchizedek who gave both bread and wine and then a blessing first, and Abram responded with a tithe. Abram didn't give a tithe to get God to bless him. He gave a tithe because God had already blessed him. It was a response to the goodness of God, not an attempt at manipulating God.

Ephesians 1:3 tells us that we have already been blessed "with every spiritual blessing in the heavenly places." God has already determined our blessings. He has already decided to give them to us. When we give to Him, we are not doing so in an effort to get from Him. We give in order to express our gratitude to Him.

We show our gratitude to God for what Jesus has secured for us as our Great High Priest. Jesus didn't pass through the three areas of the tabernacle for us. Instead, He passed through the three levels of the heavens. When He died and then rose from the grave, He ascended on a cloud and passed through the atmospheric heavens, the stellular heavens, and then into what is known as the third heavens—the throne room of God. He passed through the heavens in order to be seated on the throne at the right hand of the Father. What He has accomplished for us in this is direct access to the Father, allowing us to enter into the heavenly sanctuary to receive divine assistance, enabling us to persevere through life's challenges.

Hebrews 4:14-16 tells us what ought to be our response:

> Since we have a great high priest who has passed
> through the heavens, Jesus the Son of God, let
> us hold fast our confession. For we do not have
> a high priest who cannot sympathize with our
> weaknesses, but One who has been tempted in
> all things as we are, yet without sin. Therefore
> let us draw near with confidence to the throne
> of grace, so that we may receive mercy and find
> grace to help in time of need.

As a result of knowing Jesus as our Great High Priest, we are to hold tight to our faith. Hold fast to our confession. Not give up. Not give in. Why? Because we know we have somebody advocating for us who understands our struggles and our pain and has made a way for us to access the one who can address it.

There is no difficult category of life that anyone has ever experienced that Jesus has not also experienced. He knows what it is to be lonely. He knows what it is to be rejected. He knows what it is to be abandoned, physically beat up, hurt. He knows how it feels to cry—to weep, to shed tears of blood because the pain is so deep. He knows what it is to be betrayed. He knows what it is to be homeless. To be thirsty. Hungry. Tempted. Attacked. Spurned. Looked down upon. He even knows what it is to feel the weight of sin because, on the cross, He bore our sin. It wasn't His sin, but He bore the weight of the consequences of our own.

He can sympathize. He understands. He feels what you feel. That's why He has so much compassion. And you and

I can access that sympathy and compassion by drawing near to the throne of grace, where we receive mercy and grace to help us in our times of need. But we must take the step to draw near. We must move forward in confidence. If you have a long-distance relationship with Jesus, your Great High Priest, you will never get to witness His priesthood working on your behalf. If you are only a Sunday-morning Christian, you will never experience His priesthood helping you in your times of need. In order to see God intervene in your situations, you need to confidently approach Him through the relationship you have with Jesus, the Great High Priest. You've got to draw near.

You should never walk away from God if you are hurting. You ought to run toward Him. It's not good to stay away. You must draw near. In fact, He may even allow what you are going through to go on longer because He is trying to get you to draw near to Him. It's only as you come closer to God through the access of the Great High Priest that you can then access the grace and mercy you need.

Since Jesus occupies a throne, He can dispense divine favor (grace). And since He is our sympathetic High Priest, He can simultaneously dispense compassion (mercy). Draw near, and in so doing, you will find strength to keep going. You will find deliverance (Hebrews 7:23-25). You will find peace. You will find the Great High Priest, who will give you the help you need.

For a child will be born to us, a son will be given to us;
And the government will rest on His shoulders;
And His name will be called Wonderful Counselor,
Mighty God, Eternal Father, Prince of Peace.

ISAIAH 9:6

He is the image of the invisible God, the firstborn
of all creation. For by Him all things were created,
both in the heavens and on earth, visible and
invisible, whether thrones or dominions or rulers or
authorities—all things have been created through
Him and for Him.

COLOSSIANS 1:15-16

6

SOVEREIGN

There's a story from some years ago about a wicked storm in the Midwest. People started scrambling for shelter and, in the midst of everyone running around, a man saw a boy carrying another boy on his back. The boy being carried looked to be nearly the size of the boy carrying him, but obviously younger. The man shouted, "That boy looks heavy. Do you need help?"

To which the boy doing the carrying replied, "Oh, he's not heavy; he's my brother."

When the weight of a loved one is on your shoulders, somehow you don't feel it like you probably should. You are willing to go that extra mile—or two, or twenty—out of love. Love gives us the strength to carry others when they need us.

That same love is found in Jesus. After all, we are made in His image. We reflect His emotional DNA. But Jesus doesn't carry only one of us on His back. He carries all of us. He helps all of us. He is for all of us. Whenever we need Him. Wherever we need Him. He is there.

It's true that sometimes life can get difficult and challenging, and it may be easy to think that you are just not going to make it on your own. It's easy for all of us to think that at times. I'm not talking outside my own experience. We all need Jesus to carry us through the storms life blows our way. Which is why the name we are going to look at in this chapter is so important. Immanuel, the name we studied at the start of this book, told us that God is with us. And Jesus' positions of authority we've seen thus far, such as King, Lamb, and Great High Priest, reveal how God relates to us. But this next name gives us a glimpse into just how much God is for us—for *you*. He is on your side. He wants you to succeed. And within Himself, He has all you need in order to do so.

We uncover the concept of this name in the pages of an Old Testament passage, which is just as applicable now as it was back when it was penned.

It would be almost 700 years before the incarnation of this prophetic name would come about. It would be a long haul of difficulties, trials, and dangers for the Israelites until deity showed up in diapers. This most unique being came to fulfill a number of critical positions through His life, but a few of these can seem more personal than others. They can feel more tender than others. They might even feel more needed than others. The name hinted at in Isaiah 9:6-7, a passage which foretells the birth of Jesus, is Sovereign.

> A child will be born to us, a son will be given to
> us; and the government will rest on His shoulders;

and His name will be called Wonderful Counselor, Mighty God, Eternal Father, Prince of Peace.
There will be no end to the increase of His government or of peace, on the throne of David and
over his kingdom, to establish it and to uphold it
with justice and righteousness from then on and
forevermore. The zeal of the LORD of hosts will
accomplish this.

According to the prophet Isaiah, the child that was to be
born and the Son that was to be given would carry the weight
of the government on His shoulders. Only one entity carries the weight of the government on its shoulders, and that
entity is known as a sovereign. And while one day Jesus will
physically return to the earth and set up His rule in Jerusalem
in order to govern the whole world from Israel, He currently
holds the position of spiritual ruler over His people. The government He now actively oversees is His church and the citizens of His kingdom. Not only does He oversee us, but He
also carries us on His shoulders.

In other words, Jesus does the heavy lifting. As the Sovereign who governs the world, Jesus can bypass the red tape
of bureaucracy. When we allow Him to govern us, He carries the weight of all that needs to be maneuvered and accomplished. He provides. He connects. He arranges. He prepares.
He delivers. Unfortunately, one of the reasons why we don't
always get to experience the blessings of this role of Jesus is
that we do not allow Him to govern us or the church as a
whole. But when we do, He creates a way for us to impact
society in His name and by His strength for the glory of God
and the good of others.

But Isaiah didn't stop with just showing us Jesus' role as Sovereign. While recognizing that Jesus governs is critical, Isaiah knew that those he was writing to at that time needed to know *how* He would govern. They needed to know about the one who would deliver them for all time and in all ways—just like we do today. Which is why Isaiah gave us descriptions of how Jesus would fulfill His role of Sovereign.

Wonderful Counselor

The first governing position Isaiah shares with us in this series of descriptions is that of a counselor. Now, a counselor is someone you go to for advice. A counselor is someone you go to for guidance. If you need direction in life, you will look up a counselor. Even if you are simply looking for clarity, you can go to a counselor. A counselor does exactly what the title declares: counsels. What Isaiah reveals to us through this description is that Jesus has come to us in order to fulfill the position of extraordinary adviser. He is the great life coach. He is the Wonderful Counselor. He is for you!

Most of us have been alive long enough to have messed up sufficiently enough to realize that self-counsel sometimes works and most often doesn't. Most of us have probably experienced a time or two when the counseling we received from others just didn't seem to bring about the hoped-for result either. In fact, some counsel can leave us wondering what planet our counselor lives on. And oftentimes we can leave a session wondering if the counselor is really for us and our success, or if they're just for seeing that we come back the next week and pay again.

This is where Jesus differs.

Jesus is the Wonderful Counselor. The guidance, direction, insight, and clarity He provides is always accurate, timely, and helpful. Wisdom from above is wisdom that works. We see this repeatedly in Scripture.

- *Psalm 32:8*—"I will instruct you and teach you in the way which you should go; I will counsel you with My eye upon you."

- *Psalm 73:24*—"With Your counsel You will guide me, and afterward receive me to glory."

- *Proverbs 3:5-6*—"Trust in the LORD with all your heart and do not lean on your own understanding. In all your ways acknowledge Him, and He will make your paths straight."

- *1 Corinthians 1:25*—"The foolishness of God is wiser than men, and the weakness of God is stronger than men."

- *James 3:17*—"The wisdom from above is first pure, then peaceable, gentle, reasonable, full of mercy and good fruits, unwavering, without hypocrisy."

- *1 John 5:20*—"We know that the Son of God has come, and has given us understanding so that we may know Him who is true."

One of the reasons why life gets so distorted for us is that we lean too much on our own counsel and understanding—or we look for too many other people to give us advice. Some people even call on fortune-tellers, look to television shows, seek direction from podcasts, or find counsel from other worldly means. And while some of that can provide good, general advice some of the time, some of it clearly cannot. But even with the best podcasts or articles, the advice will be general and not as specific as what you need most to get you on the pathway to living out your destiny.

There are even people who have been messed up by counselors because they have been counseled in the wrong direction. Wrong or ill-informed counsel can stop you in your tracks. It can demolish your dreams. It can consume your hopes. In fact, it might even kill you.

When I was a young boy and suffered from repeated asthma attacks, my father would take me to the doctor to get treatment. Yet one time, the doctor made a mistake. He put the wrong medicine in the syringe. Despite his training and despite his medical wisdom, he gave me the incorrect medicine.

My dad says he still remembers that day as if it were yesterday because my reaction was so severe. They literally thought they were going to lose me. Yes, the doctor had a degree. Yes, the doctor had a license. Yes, the doctor had studied and gone to school. Yes, the doctor even charged my dad. But yes, the doctor was human. Humans make mistakes. Often, in fact.

But Jesus, the Wonderful Counselor, never makes a mistake. Ever. Colossians 2:2-3 tells us why: "Attaining to all the wealth that comes from the full assurance of understanding, resulting in a true knowledge of God's mystery, that is, Christ Himself, in whom are hidden all the treasures of wisdom and knowledge."

In Christ is hidden all wisdom and knowledge and understanding. The reason why Jesus makes such a wonderful counselor is because He knows every subject completely. What makes Him a magnificent adviser is that you cannot bring up a subject about which He doesn't possess perfect awareness and insight. Jesus doesn't merely possess perfect knowledge; He also possesses perfect understanding. Hebrews 2:17-18 tells us that He became like us so He could better help us. He's felt what you feel. He's faced rejection. He's felt scorn. He knows what it is like to be forgotten, overlooked, and underestimated. He gets it. He gets you. He understands.

Most of the time a counselor has been trained in the best counseling practices and seeks to apply those methods. But the counselor cannot always relate to how a person feels or what they have experienced. They cannot always identify with a situation personally. So while their advice might be book worthy and case-study compliant, it still often misses the mark. On the other hand, Jesus knows not only the path you should take through the twists and turns of life, but He also knows the emotional and mental roadblocks that are preventing you from overcoming what you face or reaching your goal—and how to address them. In short, He can both guide and empathize.

Jesus knows where you have come from, how you got into the situation you are in, and what you need to do in order to move forward. What's more, He also knows where all the roads of life ought to intersect and where the detours might lead you, so He can help you get to where you are going sooner rather than later. In short, He knows everything. Isaiah 40:13-14 says there is no information on earth that is beyond what God already knows. He owns the corner on counsel because He knows the end from the beginning, down from up, and everything in between.

But there are conditions to obtaining His counsel. We find one in John 7:17: "If anyone is willing to do His will, he will know of the teaching, whether it is of God." We also read in Ecclesiastes 2:26, "To a person who is good in His sight He has given wisdom and knowledge and joy." And in Proverbs 1:7, we read, "The fear of the LORD is the beginning of knowledge; fools despise wisdom and instruction." What are these conditions? Doing God's will, being good in His sight, and fearing Him. All of that can be summed up in one word: *alignment*. When you align your heart, mind, thoughts, words, and decisions under the overarching Sovereign and His rule in your life, you gain open access to His wisdom and knowledge. The firewall comes down, and you have the ability to discover God's wisdom for proper governance in and over your life.

While writing this book, I took approximately 700 people on a trip with our ministry, The Urban Alternative, to tour Israel. It had been many years since I had been to Israel, and the experience was nothing short of invigorating. Memories flooded back to me from the many trips I had taken there before. Since I had gone to Israel before, I had a general concept of the lay of the land and the geography. But in no way, shape, or form did I assign myself as the tour guide for this large group of travelers. That would have been a mistake. Rather, we partnered with a company who gives tours of Israel on a regular basis. They knew the best hotels, best roads, best food, and the best tips for navigating the country easily and comfortably.

Tour guides can make a trip run smoothly and allow you to see more than you ever could have on your own. But the only qualified tour guide for life is Jesus. There are many people who want to be your life coach, saying they are qualified to guide you, but Jesus is the only Wonderful Counselor. Jesus is your tour guide, and He does a perfect job. He never makes a mistake. Ever. Plus, He is available 24-7, 365 days out of the year. He never gets backed up. His voice mail never fills up. He never cancels appointments, goes on vacation, sleeps, or closes His doors. If you seek Him, you will find Him, because one of His roles is to make intercession for you (Hebrews 7:25).

Jesus is the Wonderful Counselor, but only if you come to Him in order to adjust what you think to what He says. Without that adjustment, He will be of no benefit to you.

Mighty God

Not only can Jesus your Sovereign give you perfect advice as your Wonderful Counselor, but He can also pull off the counsel He gives you. He has the power to see things through to completion in whatever way He directs you because He is the Mighty God.

When you take your car to the dealership, it's typically because the car is making some weird noise or some lights are on, indicating that something is wrong. Oftentimes you don't even know what is wrong yourself. You just know there is a strange sound or a light that won't turn off, and if you don't deal with the problem, it could become a much more expensive problem down the road. So you show the mechanic the light or let them hear the noise. And typically, the mechanic will fix it.

Now, the reason why you take your car to the dealership is because you do not have sufficient knowledge to fix it yourself. Unless you are a skilled do-it-yourselfer, you do not know how to make the problem right. But at the dealership, there are all types of tools to inform the mechanics on how to fix your car. They will probably start by hooking it up to a diagnostic machine to look for what is broken. Then they will do some analysis on the results, listen to the engine, look for issues that they can see, and more. In short, all these steps come together to get your car working as it should, so you can drive it back home without the noise or the annoying light.

Let me tell you something about Jesus. If you go to Him for His wonderful counsel and allow Him to perform His diagnosis on you to determine what is wrong in order to fix what is broken, He has all the tools, manpower, and might to pull it off. Jesus has the ability to calm the chaos in your life. He has the skill to rectify the confusion in your existence. He can mend your relationships and more if you will simply look to Him to do just that. See, the Mighty God is so powerful that He requires nothing outside Himself to restore everything that needs to be restored in your life.

I have a number of power strips in my home, especially in the room where we have our television and other devices. Power strips are designed to allow more than two things to be plugged into a single wall outlet. Sometimes two spots just aren't enough. And while the power to supply electricity to a number of items is available to you through an outlet, if you cannot connect those items to the outlet itself, you cannot access that power. The power strip gives you the ability to connect multiple things at one time.

Life can be similar sometimes. You may feel like you have the strength to handle an issue or two. You might feel that you can navigate through one or two trials. But when they pile up, your strength is not enough. When three, four, or five issues or difficulties mount, you simply run out of places within yourself to dig deep for that power. The Mighty God is a power strip. And He never runs out of His supply. He has enough outlets and power to handle anything and everything you are going through at any given time. The only caveat is that you need to get connected to Him.

All throughout the Gospels we see the power of this descriptive name being manifested. One example is how Jesus manifested His strength over sin. He demonstrated His ability to forgive sin and redeem people from the consequences they faced, and then urged them to go and sin no more. He also drove out demons. Healed the sick. Raised the dead. Everywhere He went, Jesus demonstrated His might and strength.

One time when Jesus met a demon-possessed man, the demons within the man confessed their name was Legion. This wasn't just one demon Jesus faced. This was an entire army of demons. Yet they were no match for the Mighty God. He drove them out, allowing them to enter a herd of unclean pigs, which then ran over the cliff to die (Luke 8:26-33). Now, what did you say your problem was? If the Mighty God can handle an entire legion of demons, He has enough power to help you overcome whatever it is you are facing.

In fact, even the devil must first go to God. He had to ask permission to touch Job (see Job 1:6-12). He also had to ask God in order to tempt and challenge Peter—to "sift" him like wheat (Luke 22:31). We give the devil far too much credit. Jesus not only has greater power, but He also has entire authority. He can overrule anything you need Him to—any circumstance, whether physical, emotional, or spiritual. He is the Mighty God, the divine Sovereign, and He is for you.

Eternal Father

The third name for Jesus given to us in Isaiah 9:6 is Eternal Father. This name is probably the one which is least likely to be used by any of us for Jesus. The reason for this is because we often distinguish between God the Father and Jesus the Son, while forgetting that Jesus is the exact representation of the Father (Hebrews 1:3). He is the reflection of God in the flesh (John 10:30,38). And while Isaiah was not making the claim that Jesus *is* the first person of the Trinity, God the Father (the early church denounced this as the heresy of modalism), He was pointing out a character quality of Jesus that reflects the Father. In this sense, Jesus is fatherly and offers those attributes of fatherhood to us.

To help you see this more clearly, let me give an example from my own life. As a pastor and counselor, and also as a radio preacher, I will often get called "Father" by people who are not my biological or adopted children. I'm called a

spiritual father or simply Father. In fact, I even have people who are older than me call me Father sometimes. Now, it's not that I am replacing their biological fathers in any way; they are simply using a term that most accurately reflects the nature of our relationship. In some way, they feel that I have fathered them.

When Isaiah called Jesus by this name, He wanted us to see that Jesus embodies more than just attributes of redemption, rule, and righteousness. He wanted us to recognize that Jesus is a father to us in many ways, whether by guiding, leading, giving, encouraging, or protecting those of us under His care.

Yet the name Eternal Father gives us more than just insight into Jesus' fatherly care. It is also an intentional reminder that Jesus sits outside time as the originator of time. As the Alpha and the Omega, He knows no beginning or end (Revelation 1:8). Or, as Isaiah recorded elsewhere, "Thus says the high and exalted One who lives forever, whose name is Holy" (Isaiah 57:15). God lives forever. Each person of the Trinity is not constrained by time. As the second member of the Trinity, Jesus sits as an overseer of history and a regulator of time. Hebrews 1:10-12 tells us that Jesus existed before time, in a world without time. And while we may live in a continuum from A to Z and birth to death, Jesus does not. He is not bound by our reality nor constrained within our measurements. He is eternal. He is everlasting. He has no beginning, and He will have no end.

I understand that this description of Jesus is one of the more difficult ones to comprehend because we only know the existence of time. Ecclesiastes 3:1-8 tells us that, in the world in which we live, there is a time for everything—whether to laugh, cry, live, or die. We are clothed with time. Some may even say we are trapped in time. There is no way to escape it. You and I are getting older by the day. We are getting grayer by the year. Why? Because we are in a closed universe with our very lives contingent upon the passing of time.

But Jesus sits outside time. He governs time. He is Sovereign. And as we often refer to the fictional Mother Nature as a controller of seasons and weather patterns, we see in this description that Jesus truly is Father Time. He is our Eternal Father.

It is in recognizing Him in this position that you can discover how to make the most of your time. When He is allowed to govern your time, He can guide it, intersect it, connect it, organize it, use it, oversee it, and help you pass through it in such a way that you have all you need when you need it.

What God is revealing to us through this prophetic name given thousands of years ago is that if we will allow Jesus to govern our time, He can provide the insight we need to use it the way we should. Ephesians 5:15-16 instructs us concerning time: "Be careful how you walk, not as unwise men but as wise, making the most of your time, because the days are evil." Jesus is our loving Eternal Father who wants to see us use our time in such a way that we maximize it for the glory of God and the good of others. He, like any wise father, desires that you learn how to maneuver through time as best you can in order to experience the fullest life you can possibly have. And He knows exactly how to guide you, instruct you, and motivate you to do just that.

Prince of Peace

Lastly, Isaiah wants us to know that Jesus is our Prince of Peace. The Hebrew word for *peace* is *shalom*. If you were to visit Israel, you would hear "shalom" used as a form of greeting all the time. It's a pregnant word, containing much more than our contemporary understanding of the term *peace*. The concept of *shalom* is wellness or being well ordered. So when a Jewish person says "Shalom" to you when they greet you, they are not just telling you they hope you are happy. They are saying they hope your life is put together in order. In English, that would mean "no more drama." It means that life is intact.

If we were to translate this name into a modern American context, it might read "Prince of No More Drama." Jesus is the Prince of Calm. He is the deliverer from chaos and confusion.

Now, it's true—life comes with drama. It just does. We can expect bad days. They come with living on a fallen earth with fallen humanity. But peace would be a rare commodity indeed if we had to depend on our circumstances as our only source for that peace. Yet this name reminds us that we have a far better source. In fact, Jesus is the only true source. He stated this clearly: "I have told you these things so that in Me you may have peace. You will have suffering in this world. Be courageous! I have conquered the world" (John 16:33 HCSB). Jesus has the power to invoke peace even in the midst of our most frightening situations.

I have been on the Sea of Galilee numerous times. On one trip, the guide told our group that the location of the Sea of Galilee in the Jordan Rift causes tempests to flare up violently with little or no notice. A tempest like that could be daunting, and the one the disciples encountered in the story recorded in

Mark 4:35-41 took place at night. Clouds would have hidden any light from the moon. In the dark of night, out in the middle of the sea, the storm surely must have caught the disciples off guard. The storm tested not only their boating expertise, but also their emotions. When reading this passage, I can feel their fear. I can see Peter drenched to the bone, along with the rest of the disciples, on this tempestuous sea. I'm not surprised that they woke up Jesus and asked Him, "Don't You care that we're going to die?" (verse 38 HCSB). I probably would have done the same thing. In fact, I can't really see Peter simply asking the question; I picture him yelling it.

"Jesus, don't You care that we are about to die? Wake up!"

Jesus responded calmly to the disciples' desperate cry. He got up from His slumber, faced the storm, and spoke to the sea, "Silence! Be still!" (verse 39 HCSB). Two brief commands, and the storm obeyed. The Greek word for *silence* comes from the root word *siópé*, which literally means "hold your peace." In essence, Jesus told the storm to be quiet. To stop its noise. To hush its fuss. Similar to a parent correcting an unruly toddler, Jesus told the sea to "settle down."

It was as simple and as immediate as that. Scripture tells us, "There was a great calm" (verse 39 HCSB). Peace had come.

Friend, thunder and lightning might be chasing each other all around you. The wind could be blowing unexpected and unpleasant circumstances into your life. Nothing looks right. Nothing looks promising. All is pitch-black at night. But it is precisely in those times that Jesus' peace triumphs in the storm. With a simple word from His lips, He speaks peace into your present situation.

Let's face it. Peace is hard to come by for most of us. But when you come to know this name of Jesus in an intimate way, peace is yours for the taking.

Have you ever flown in a plane in the middle of a storm? I have. Cups spilled, overhead compartments burst open, and people screamed all around me. I've never been one to be afraid of flying, but in those times, even the stoutest among us buckle up and pay attention.

The story is told of a flight that hit some unusual turbulence, tossing the airplane side to side in strong gusts of wind. Clouds looked more like coal. Lightning danced nearby. An eerie silence settled over the passengers in between their shrieks and screams. No one felt safe.

Except for one small child, that is. He sat there, preoccupied with his notebook and pen, drawing a picture of himself climbing a tree on a sun-filled day. To look at him, no one ever would have guessed he was on a plane in the middle of a storm.

A passenger nearby noticed him and wondered how he could feel so calm, so she asked the young boy, "Aren't you afraid?"

He just looked up from his paper for a moment, smiled, and said, "No."

"Why not?" the lady prodded, fingers gripping her seat.

"Because my dad is the pilot," he answered matter-of-factly, then returned to his drawing.

I get it. I understand that sometimes life seems out of control. It's easy to feel afraid. But knowing the Prince of Peace sits at the controls ought to usher in a heart of peace.

The word *peace* gets used a lot, but we often misunderstand its real meaning. In a war-torn area, peace stands for something more like a truce bringing a temporary reprieve. To a young mother, it could stand for that hour when the toddlers take their naps.

Peace means different things to different people. But the kind Jesus offers is like no other. His peace produces internal calm in the midst of external chaos. We experience His peace when we trade in our fears of the storm for a healthy fear and reverence of Him. When we shift our gaze from the sea to the Savior, peace ensues.

Paul told us to respond to God's peace the same way the storm responded to Jesus that night on the Sea of Galilee. "Let the peace of the Messiah...control your hearts" (Colossians 3:15 HCSB). The Greek word used for *control* means "to umpire." We all know what an umpire does. He declares the way things are. Whatever he says the result is—a ball, a strike, an out, or a run—that's what it is.

Likewise, whatever the Prince of Peace says about a matter, that's what it is. It's settled because He is sovereign in His decisions.

Friend, your world may be falling apart, but you don't have to fall apart with it. You can't always control what happens to you or into what storms you may fly, but you do have control over how you respond. Responding to Jesus' presence and power in your life allows you to let go of your fear and replace it with peace—His peace. This doesn't mean you won't have problems, but it does mean your problems won't have you.

Relationships may falter. Jobs may cease. Health may decline. The economy could continue to dip and turn. But

Jesus says, "Silence! Be still!" You can rest comfortably on your cushion, because the Prince of Peace has got you in His hands.[3] God wants to establish a covenant of peace with you (Ezekiel 34:25; 37:26).

I'm sure you have seen an orchestra tuning up for a concert at some point, whether live or on TV or the internet. During this time, it sounds like chaos. Musical instruments blast out their sounds with no rhyme or reason. But when the conductor walks to the stage and raises his baton, his presence changes everything. Everyone is now focused on him. And what was once chaos somehow transforms into a harmonious score.

When Jesus is allowed to govern your life as the true Sovereign—Wonderful Counselor, Mighty God, Eternal Father, and Prince of Peace—whatever was once chaotic in your life will adjust to Him. It will become harmonious when He is allowed to serve as ruler and arranger over all. Soon you will discover that all of your life is lining up in order. But that only happens when you align yourself under Him. These benefits, as displayed through His names, come to you when you are in tune with Him, following His direction and sovereign authority. There is peace where God rules (Isaiah 52:7).

In Jesus' names, you find counsel, power, direction, and peace. In Him, you find everything you need. Therefore, you must give Jesus the sovereign right to govern every aspect of your life so that the benefits of His rule become more than a theological description—they become a personal experience.

PART 2

POWER IN HIS PERSON

God said to Moses, "I AM WHO I AM."

Exodus 3:14

Jesus said to them, "Truly, truly, I say to you, before Abraham was born, I am."

John 8:58

7

I AM

Jesus is God's selfie. Most of us know what a selfie is in our culture today, but in case you don't, a selfie is when someone takes a picture of himself or herself. Pretty self-explanatory (no pun intended). Now, a selfie can include other people in the photo, but it has to include the one taking the picture. If someone else takes a photo of a person, it can't be considered a selfie. Why? Because a selfie always reflects the image of the person taking the photo.

Jesus is God's selfie in that He is the exact representation and manifestation of God Himself. He isn't just a friend. He isn't part of a group hopping into the photo. Jesus is God's selfie.

God is invisible to us in His essence. Our finite being cannot comprehend or see Him; the sight would vaporize us. Without Jesus, we cannot know God's heart, His person, or His character intimately because He is wholly other and sits outside our realm of understanding. But out of God's great love for us, He desired to be known by us. He wanted to be seen by us. So, in order to do that, He had to come to us in a form we would be able to understand. He had to be both man and God simultaneously, which—although this gave us a greater glimpse into who God is—created a larger gap for those who would not believe.

In John 8:48-59, we come across my favorite name of Jesus: I Am. When Jesus introduced this name to the world at this moment in history, He drew many in closer to God—but He also pushed many more away. This is a name you cannot halfway embrace. Either Jesus is I Am, or He is a liar. You may think that is a harsh word to use, but Jesus Himself said He would be a liar if He claimed not to know the Father (verses 54-55).

The name I Am shows up in the midst of a heated discussion. Not long before, Jesus had forgiven the adulterous woman and driven away a number of angry, hypocritical, judgmental men who sought to stone her. His miracles of healing and driving out demons had given Him a reputation by this time. Jesus was someone to be reckoned with, yet not everyone knew how to place Him. Was He a good man doing good things? Was He of the devil using demonic powers? Was He...God?

Consider for a moment how Jesus must have felt during this heated discussion that we read about in John 8:48-59. Jews encircled Him and pounded Him with questions and accusations. Words quickly became harsh. Some accused Him of having a demon. To which Jesus unloaded a soliloquy of sorts, a somewhat personal reflection that was also for the benefit of others. After all, Jesus was speaking to those He came to redeem. The sins He would carry on the cross were their sins. Not only that, but the blood that coursed through their veins was blood He created. The skin that held their organs in place was skin He held together. The air they breathed was air He made and preserved each and every day. It was His genius that had prepared a place where humanity could live, food could be produced, and regeneration could occur. It was His strength that held the stars at bay so they would not tumble too closely and destroy the planet. His energy infused the sun. He gave life to each person standing there, the ones nodding in agreement that He might have a demon in Him.

It's one thing to be insulted by someone who doesn't know you. Maybe you can identify. If someone you barely know on social media or a casual acquaintance mocks you, that's one level of pain. But when the very people you sustain—either through caregiving, provision, or some other way—insult you, it's difficult to contain the feelings of outright pain.

No doubt Jesus' words came peppered with an extra bit of spice when He rebuked His accusers that day. It's surprising that He didn't just raise His hand and make them all fall instantly to the ground. How dare they even insinuate that the one who gave them the ability to speak is less than they are, as lowly and unrighteous as a demon.

But Jesus exercised power in His self-control. I would have loved to have seen the look in His eyes and hear the lengthened breath He took when He replied, "I do not have a demon." Perhaps He looked down at that point. Perhaps He looked up.

Perhaps He stared right into the souls of His accusers. Whatever the case, I imagine He could have pierced the core of the earth with His gaze when He continued, "I honor My Father, and you dishonor Me" (John 8:49).

Jesus continued the dialogue a bit longer. Accusations kept coming. His responses showed restraint coupled with intentionality. Until, ultimately, He left it all on the table. The Jews around Him mocked Him by jesting, "You are not yet fifty years old, and have You seen Abraham?" And He did not hold back. His reply revealed all. I can almost hear His voice softening, growing patient like a parent with a child who simply will not understand. "Truly, truly, I say to you, before Abraham was born, I am" (verses 57-58).

He knew that statement would end the conversation. And, in fact, it did. The Jews picked up stones to kill Him, but He hid from them. Why would people pick up stones to kill someone who made that statement? Because the word *am* is in the present tense. Jesus didn't say, "Before Abraham was, I was." No, He let them know that before Abraham was, He *is*. He exists in the eternal present tense, and only one being can claim that: God Himself.

This assertion sent the Jews into the ionosphere of anger because, to them, that was nothing short of blasphemy. See, when Jesus identified with the name I Am, it took His listeners all the way back to Exodus 3. They knew exactly what He was saying because Jewish culture in that day required a detailed understanding of the Scriptures.

> Moses said to God, "Behold, I am going to the
> sons of Israel, and I will say to them, 'The God of

your fathers has sent me to you.' Now they may
say to me, 'What is His name?' What shall I say to
them?" God said to Moses, "I AM WHO I AM";
and He said, "Thus you shall say to the sons of
Israel, 'I AM has sent me to you'" (verses 13-14).

Thus, the reason rocks flew when Jesus declared He was I
Am is because He outright declared He was God. As the designated spokesman of the Trinity (the Word of God), Jesus was
stating that He was the one speaking from the bush to Moses
way back when.

The name I Am is called the *tetragrammaton*. That's a theological word that simply means "the four letters." I Am is comprised of four consonants in the Hebrew language. Originally,
the Hebrew language was written in abjad (a form of symbolic
writing), meaning it did not have any vowels. Seeing as how
this name of God has no vowels, it could not be pronounced
exactly as it was written. This is because there is simply no way
to recite four consonants as a word itself. In order to talk about
God, one must insert vowels into the name YHWH. This
becomes Yahweh in written format.[4] We know it as Jehovah
in the English language. In Scripture, this name is often written as LORD in small caps. The meaning of this name is "the
covenant-keeping relational God."

Now, all this talk of names, translations of names, pronun-
ciations of names, speaking of names, and writing of names
can get confusing. But it's critical for us to fully comprehend
this because identity and character are tied to names, especially God's names. God has many different names in Scripture. Each one is designed to describe a different aspect of who

He is and what He does. For example, the name applied to Him with regard to creation and the formation of all things is Elohim. When we read the name Adonai, that refers to God as "boss" and "ruler." And when God chose to relate to humanity in a more personal context, He gave us the name YHWH (Yahweh or Jehovah). He took this name—the same name Jesus presented as His own (I Am, YHWH)—when He sought to explain who He was in relationship to mankind. We shouldn't be surprised, then, that Jesus used this relational name in revealing who He was to those around Him at that time. Seeing as He left heaven for the direct purpose of relating to us on earth, He offered us all, in this setting, the one name that described Him best.

When we break down the composition of the name I Am, we get a closer look at the heart of God. It signifies His loyal, covenant-keeping character. The first word in this name is *I*, and *I* is a personal pronoun. This tells us that it is the person himself talking, and in calling Himself by this name, God is indicating that He wants to relate to us personally. God is not only interested in being the big mahoff way up there; He also wants to talk to us down here, where we live. In other words, we are able to communicate with Him personally.

Not only is this name personal, but it is also indicative of the present tense. *Am* is not past tense ("was"), nor is it future tense ("will be"). What this explains to us is that God has no past, and He has no future. He has no yesterday, and He has no tomorrow. Everything about God is *now*. He simply *is*.

It's difficult for us to relate to this truth or comprehend it because we live our lives linearly. We progress from one to ten.

That's just how we live because we exist in time and space. But God lives outside time and space. He *is*. He always has been *is*. And He always will be *is*. I know this is beyond our human comprehension, but God sits outside the minds He gave us with which to understand and live. Yet in trying to understand as much as we can about this name, we become assured of a few things.

First, whatever God has prophesied for the future, we may be waiting on, but He is not. He is always in the present tense. That's why you and I can bank on anything He says, because what He declares will happen has already happened in His existence. He's not hoping it will happen. He knows it already has.

Second, this name gives us insight into God's totality. When He declared who He was to Moses, He said, "I AM WHO I AM" (Exodus 3:14). Essentially, He defined Himself by Himself. He did not and does not need anyone else to define Him. This relates to us today in that He is not what we want Him to be. He is not what we demand Him to be. He is who He is, the self-defining God. Our perspective on who we think He should be doesn't matter at all. It leads to numerous misconceptions about God when humanity seeks to define Him according to our terms.

Third, I Am exists as an eternal being, not changing in nature. Hebrews 13:8 says it this way: "Jesus Christ is the same yesterday and today and forever." We can't say the same of ourselves. Not even close. Have you ever looked back at old photos of yourself and wondered what on earth happened? Or have you gone to a high school reunion and not been able to recognize people you had been friends with years earlier? Why? People change. We all change. We are rarely the same even a day later. But Jesus is not like that. Jesus is eternally present and eternally the same. It is built into the nature of God to be who He is and not change. Just as water is wet, the sun is hot, and the sky is blue by their very nature, even so Jesus' nature and essential being are forever unchanged.

James 1:17 says, "Every good thing given and every perfect gift is from above, coming down from the Father of lights, with whom there is no variation or shifting shadow." He does not change. Yes, the Bible talks about Him changing His mind or changing His approach. But He never changes His essence. He stays the same person, even when He changes His methodology. And much of the change in His methods depends on us. Our changes and adjustments to Him will often affect how He relates to us—but that is because we are now relating to another aspect of who He is.

Maybe it will help to explain it this way. The sun does not change. It is planet Earth that rotates around the sun. Half of the earth is dark at any given time, not because the sun changes, but because the earth's relationship to the sun changes. Seasons change. Weather patterns change. But none of that happens because the sun has changed. It all happens because of the earth's movement and its proximity to the sun. It is the earth that has adjusted, not the sun.

Similarly, when we adjust to God or move in proximity to Him, it may look like He's changed because the results of our relationship with Him change, but He Himself has not changed. We are merely tapping into an aspect of Him that is different from what we encountered before because we have moved. Which is why repentance is so critical in your experience of God. Repentance means you turn from what is causing distance between you and God, and then you turn toward what pleases God. This draws you into a closer proximity with Him, and you experience various aspects of His character in different ways.

When Jesus stated, "I am," He let those around Him know that He is the personal, present, powerful, unfaltering, self-contained God.

And stones flew.

But Jesus didn't stop there. In fact, seven times in the book of John, Jesus referred to Himself as I Am. In each reference, He designated a different aspect of who He is and how He relates to us.

- "I am the bread of life; he who comes to Me will not hunger, and he who believes in Me will never thirst" (6:35).

- "I am the Light of the world; he who follows Me will not walk in the darkness, but will have the Light of life" (8:12).

- "Truly, truly, I say to you, I am the door of the sheep" (10:7).

- "I am the good shepherd; the good shepherd lays down His life for the sheep...I am the good shepherd, and I know My own and My own know Me" (10:11,14).

- "I am the resurrection and the life; he who believes in Me will live even if he dies" (11:25).

- "I am the way, and the truth, and the life; no one comes to the Father but through Me" (14:6).

- "I am the true vine, and My Father is the vine-dresser…I am the vine, you are the branches; he who abides in Me and I in him, he bears much fruit, for apart from Me you can do nothing" (15:1,5).

Let's look at each of these references individually to glean from them Jesus' power for our lives.

I Am the Bread of Life

This name stems from the Old Testament, when the Israelites were wandering in the wilderness. If you are familiar with the story, you know that to assuage their hunger, God sent down bread from heaven. These "cornflakes" from above, tiny wafers that literally floated from the sky, were known as manna. For six days of the week, the Israelites could eat their fill of manna. On the sixth day, they had to store enough to eat on the seventh day, which was a day of rest (see Exodus 16).

When Jesus said He Himself is the bread of life, able to satisfy both our hunger and our thirst, He was letting us know that He is the fulfillment of all we need spiritually. Just as the body gets hungry, so does the soul. When you know Jesus personally and abide in Him fully, your soul has no lack.

Do you know what it is like to have hot bread come out of the oven when you are hungry, and you get some butter and jelly to put on it? You probably start drooling a bit before you even bite into it. This bread satisfies you deeply. Satisfaction is available to each of us when we come to know this name of Jesus. He is substance for our souls, and He is also our delight. But we only access this when we make Him our life, when we become absorbed in Him.

Many of the problems we face today come about because our souls are starving while our bellies are full. Our souls are empty while our bank accounts are full. Many defeats, addictions, and relational crises occur due to empty souls. Which is why far too many people stay miserable for far too long. Only Jesus can deliver true satisfaction to satiate our hunger and our thirst. There is no place you can go, no vacation you can take, no person you can talk to that can fill the gap only He can fill. Our problems arise because we are hungering or thirsting for everything else but Jesus. Matthew 5:6 tells us there is only one way to be satisfied: "Blessed are those who hunger and thirst for righteousness, for they shall be satisfied."

I Am the Light of the World

Not only does Jesus feed you, but He also illuminates you. He told us this so we would know that when we follow Him, He will allow us to see where we are going. The proof that many of us do not know this name of Jesus or apply its power in our lives is that it is obvious we don't know where we are going. We keep going down the wrong path and making wrong decisions. But Jesus says when we come to know Him in a close, abiding manner, He gives us light. He illuminates our walkways. He supplies wisdom for our decisions.

But unless you follow Jesus, you will walk in darkness. You will live spiritually blind. To be physically blind is a great hindrance. Spiritual blindness is even more life-shattering. Spiritual blindness leads to confusion and a lack of clarity. Illumination provides direction, connection, and power. When you access His light, you access all you need to see everywhere you need to go.

I Am the Door of the Sheep

This "I am" offers entrance. Every shepherd has a gate. This is a door through which the sheep can enter. John 10:9 says, "I am the door; if anyone enters through Me, he will be saved, and will go in and out and find pasture." This door grants us entrance into heaven—but also more than heaven. We read in this verse that we can go in and out. Thus, through Jesus we discover freedom and good pasture here on earth. Yet this only happens when we access Jesus as the door. We can't go around Jesus to get to good pasture. We can't skip Jesus to find freedom. If we want to make our way to a place of deep satisfaction, we must go through the door, through Jesus. He is the I Am who offers fullness of life.

Verse 10 tells us even more. "The thief comes only to steal and kill and destroy; I came that they may have life, and have it abundantly." Jesus came and died, then rose again, not so that you and I could just possess life, but so that we could have abundant life. He desires us to experience the fullness of life.

Friend, you are to have super-life. And the way you obtain this is through abiding in this name of Jesus. It is in understanding that He not only illuminates the pathways of life, but that He also grants access to those pathways as the door, that you will come to understand He is all and over all. He is the centerpiece of all true and lasting satisfaction.

I Am the Good Shepherd

Not only does a shepherd open the door for the sheep to enter, but a good shepherd also watches over his sheep. He is responsible for them. If anything happens to the sheep, it is the shepherd who is blamed—not the sheep. Sheep are entirely dependent upon the shepherd to guide them where they need to go and to keep them safe.

See, sheep are some of the dumbest animals ever created. They are so dumb that they will follow one another even when they are only going around in circles. They aren't known for being the brightest creatures on the block. Which is why we are compared to them in Isaiah 53:6: "All of us like sheep have gone astray, each of us has turned to his own way; but the LORD has caused the iniquity of us all to fall on Him."

When Jesus is our shepherd, He can lead us where we need to go. Psalm 23 paints another picture of this.

> The LORD is my shepherd,
> I shall not want.
> He makes me lie down in green pastures;
> He leads me beside quiet waters.
> He restores my soul;
> He guides me in the paths of righteousness
> For His name's sake.
> Even though I walk through the valley of the
> shadow of death,

> I fear no evil, for You are with me;
> Your rod and Your staff, they comfort me.
> You prepare a table before me in the presence of
> my enemies;
> You have anointed my head with oil;
> My cup overflows.
> Surely goodness and lovingkindness will follow
> me all the days of my life,
> And I will dwell in the house of the Lord
> forever.

The name that is translated "Lord" in Psalm 23 is the name we've been looking at in this chapter: YHWH. Jesus is the ever-present, relational being who takes care of us in every single area of life. He takes care of our directional needs, leading us in the paths of righteousness. He takes care of our spiritual well-being, causing us to lie down in green pastures. He takes care of our emotional needs, helping us fear no evil when we walk through the valley. He also takes care of our physical needs, anointing our heads with oil and making our cups run over in abundance. And, on top of all that, He takes care of our eternal needs, having goodness and mercy follow us all the days of our life and allowing us to ultimately dwell in the house of the Lord forever.

As the great I Am, Jesus has your back directionally, spiritually, emotionally, physically, and eternally. He is your source for all you need. And He knows exactly what you need and when you need it.

I Am the Resurrection and the Life

Jesus spoke these words to a broken friend in the face of her brother's death. Lazarus had just died. Martha had lost hope. She had momentarily forgotten how to believe. Grief can do that to you, can't it? It can cover you with clouds so thick that you no longer recognize where you are. But Jesus comforted Martha in her moment of pain. He reminded her of the ultimate truth that He is the resurrection and the life (see John 11:17-27).

Jesus reminded Martha—and all of us—that when it comes to grief and death, you need more than theology on a shelf. You need Him. Just like when you are sick, you don't need a medical book or a medical research page on the internet—you need a doctor who is going to give you medicine. When you are in trouble, you don't need a law book—you need a lawyer. You need the incarnation of the book.

Jesus came that He might give life, but He also came as the life itself. He is the power of resurrection, and He is life. When you allow life's troubles and trials to drive you to Him, you will come to recognize His power not only to calm you in the midst of chaos, but also to resurrect those things in your life which you thought—beyond a shadow of a doubt—were dead.

I Am the Way, and the Truth, and the Life

Most of us go through our lives hoping we know where we are going. We spend money on fancy apps to help us navigate through the maze of life like a pro. But try visiting a foreign country or a location where road construction is taking place, and you can no longer depend on your apps. You'll quickly discover how important knowing the way to where you are going truly is. But this not only applies to directions for a physical destination; it also applies to where you are heading in life—in your career, family, hopes, and destiny.

Now, in John 14:6, Jesus didn't just tell us that He knows the way. He told us that He *is* the way. You and I no longer have to guess. He is our GPS, and the location is Him. When we abide in Him and align ourselves under Him, He takes us where we need to go. He opens those doors we didn't even have the ability to knock on. He removes those people who sought to remove us first. He overcomes the obstacles our emotions may throw in our path. He calms the corners that look too difficult to handle on our own. He is the way.

Not only that, but He is also the truth. Now, don't skim over that. I didn't say He is *a* truth. And Jesus Himself didn't say He is *a* truth. Rather, He is *the* truth. All truth is rooted in Jesus alone. And unless your truth, or your friends' truth, or the media's truth agrees with His truth, it's just not true. Far too many people believe a lie because they follow a "truth" outside *the* truth, Jesus Christ.

No one can decide that one plus one equals eleven just because they want it to. It will never equal eleven, no matter how many people want to say it does. Truth is truth. It is objective. And it is founded in Christ Himself. If you choose to live your life according to anything other than Jesus' truth, you will face the consequences that result.

There is an absolute standard by which all else is measured. There is an absolute standard on the definition of the beginning of life. There is an absolute standard on the definition of marriage. Same for racial issues. Same for helping the poor. And on and on. Jesus is the standard, and He has spoken. Without living according to His way and His truth, you will lack life. The only way to access the life He died to give you here on earth—the abundant life—is to follow His path according to His truth.

I Am the True Vine

Jesus is the real deal. He is the authentic one. Anything and everything else are cheap substitutes. In order to access His power, though, you must abide in Him. Since He is the vine that supplies life to the fruit, your work is to remain in Him. It is when you rest in Him that He does His work both in and through you.

Far too often today, people live for themselves. They make it all about them. In the realm of fruit bearing, that would be called rotten fruit. Only rotten fruit eats itself. Jesus desires that you abide in Him, the true vine, so you will bear fruit that will benefit others. When you reflect Him, as fruit always reflects the vine from which it grows, you will become a conduit of Christ's life to those around you. But this can only happen through abiding. This can only come about when you let go of your efforts, your goals, and your own strength, and instead rest in the true vine, which supplies you with all you need to live out your destiny.

He Is Everything You Need

Friend, when you come to know these seven descriptions of Jesus residing within the name I Am and look to Him, you

will experience the full manifestation of His power and presence both in and through you. When God revealed this name
to Moses at the burning bush, He also revealed to him his calling. He gave Moses his purpose. It was then that He told him
to go to Pharaoh and tell Pharaoh to let His people go. God
gave Moses a reason for living, and this reason was bigger than
anything he could have done on his own (see Exodus 3:10-22).

When you seek to enter the presence of Jesus in such a way
that you humble yourself under this great name, you will discover the plans He has for you—plans that will blow your mind.
Not only that, but you will also discover—as Moses did when
he threw down his rod and picked it back up again (Exodus
4:1-5)—the power He has for you to carry out those plans.

Psalm 9:10 tells us, "Those who know Your name will put
their trust in You, for You, O LORD, have not forsaken those
who seek You." When you get to know the names of Jesus, you
discover on whom you can base your truth. He will not for-
sake you when you seek Him with your whole heart and mind.
There is power in the name of Jesus. John 18:4-6 gives a rare,
tangible look at this power.

> Jesus, knowing all the things that were coming
> upon Him, went forth and said to them, "Whom
> do you seek?" They answered Him, "Jesus the
> Nazarene." He said to them, "I am He." And
> Judas also, who was betraying Him, was standing
> with them. So when He said to them, "I am He,"
> they drew back and fell to the ground.

When Jesus said, "I am He," the soldiers literally had to
back away and fall to the ground.

I don't know what is after you or what situation threatens you. I don't know what difficulty you might be facing right now. But I do know this: When you know the great I Am, all of those challenges have to back away. There is power in Jesus' name.

A story goes that a little girl's father came to her one day and encouraged her to open up a bank account with the allowance she had been receiving. So the little girl agreed and opened up an account. She was then given the ability to purchase things from her account online through the use of her bank card.

One day the little girl came to her daddy crying. When he asked her what was wrong, she replied, "Daddy, Daddy, the bank is going broke. You picked a bad bank."

The father considered what she was saying for a minute. Then he asked her, "Why do you think the bank is going broke?"

She replied, "Because when I try to buy another game online, it says, 'Error, insufficient funds.'"

That's when the father smiled and assured his daughter that the bank was not going broke at all. The bank had more than enough money to cover anything and everything she wanted to buy. The problem was that she hadn't deposited enough money in her account to cover the purchase.

Friend, if the account of your life reads "insufficient joy," "insufficient peace," "insufficient power," "insufficient order," and more, it is not because the bank in heaven is empty. No, it's because you are not depositing the honor, worship, and commitment to Jesus that is required to access all He has in store for you. After all, His name is I Am. And I Am means that He is everything you need. He is whatever it is you are lacking. He is whatever it is you need Him to be. But you need to get to know Him more fully, seek Him more passionately, and align yourself under Him more intentionally to access the benefits of His names.

*If you confess with your mouth Jesus as Lord, and
believe in your heart that God raised Him from the
dead, you will be saved.*

Romans 10:9

*So that at the name of Jesus every knee shall bow, of
those who are in heaven and on earth and under
the earth, and that every tongue will confess that
Jesus Christ is Lord, to the glory of God the Father.*

Philippians 2:10-11

8

LORD

Have you ever watched cable television only to have the channel go out and the words "searching for signal" appear on your screen? That's what happens to many believers who do not know this next name of Jesus we are going to explore.

Oftentimes, people feel the name Lord is just something to throw into their prayers to make them sound more spiritual. Or something to add to a conversation to give the impression of a high level of holiness. But this name carries with it much more than semantic illusions. It carries authority.

Now, I'm not saying believers have been cut off from accessing any authority endowed through the sacrifice of Jesus. But when we do not know this name or how to rightfully relate to it while on earth, we experience an interruption in the signal. The enemy has been allowed to somehow interfere with the communication and alignment we have with Jesus. So even if you or I have the best 4K television on the market, all we get is static.

In order to gain access to what the name Lord supplies, we first have to understand the difference between two terms. Far too often we confuse them and wind up losing the spiritual battles we face.

God has given His Son ultimate authority over what happens in history. He has placed all things in subjection to Him. As we read in Ephesians, "He put all things in subjection under His feet, and gave Him as head over all things to the church, which is His body, the fullness of Him who fills all in all" (1:22-23).

One of the reasons we often don't live in light of this truth is because we confuse the terms *power* and *authority*. Satan has power. He dominates the world in which we live and influences people's lives in countless ways. He is as powerful now as he has ever been. His tactics and destruction are both real and damaging. But what he doesn't have is final authority. Authority is the right to use the power you possess.

For example, football players are generally bigger and stronger—more powerful—than the referees. The referees are often older, smaller, and more out of shape than the players. The players can knock someone down. That's called power. But the referees can put someone out of a game. That's called authority.

See, Satan has power, but the only way he is free to use that power over you is through your failure to operate in alignment with Jesus as Lord. Satan does not have the authority to use his power when you function under the covenantal covering of the Lord.

This is why Satan will try so hard and long to lure you away from the lordship of Jesus Christ. He knows that if he can get you out from under His covering, he has free reign to deceive, trick, and harm you however he chooses. It is under the covering of the lordship of Christ that you stand protected.

Two Kingdoms

Colossians 1:13 tells us that God has "rescued us from the domain of darkness, and transferred us to the kingdom of His beloved Son." God rescued us from the authority of darkness and out of the wrong kingdom. By rescuing us, He transferred us to live our lives under the rule of a new King, the Lord Jesus Christ. As believers, we used to belong to Satan's kingdom and rulership before meeting the Lord, but now we are part of a new kingdom where Jesus Christ is the King. Satan, in order to rule the lives and institutions of kingdom followers, has got to get us to leave the Lord's kingdom rule and come back over to his.

Much of this happens through the division of the secular and the sacred. This is done when people attend and participate in church under one kingdom, then go out into the world Monday through Saturday and function under the influence of another kingdom. We do Bible studies in one kingdom and socialize under the influence of unrighteous friends in another kingdom. Essentially, we experience this flip-flop of kingdoms and then wonder why there is not more victory in our life.

The answer is simple. Satan is ruling people's lives because they are yielding the power to him—not by way of any rightful authority he has, but simply because they fail to align their thoughts and decisions under the Lord. When we abandon the union we were created to have with Christ under His headship as Lord, authority is lost. By not giving the Lord His proper place in our home, our church, and our world—the place He deserves—we lose His covering. All life for a kingdom follower ought to be lived in recognition of the lordship of Jesus Christ.

> He is the image of the invisible God, the firstborn of all creation. For by Him all things were created, both in the heavens and on earth, visible and invisible, whether thrones or dominions or rulers or authorities—all things have been created through Him and for Him. He is before all things, and in Him all things hold together. He is also head of the body, the church; and He is the beginning, the firstborn from the dead, so that He Himself will come to have first place in everything (Colossians 1:15-18).

With the resurrection and exaltation of Jesus Christ, He has been made head over all rulers and authorities. He is in charge. When a person accepts Jesus as their sin bearer, then they have transferred kingdoms. Jesus is then to be preeminent in their life—He is to have first place in all things. Only as the lordship of Christ is acknowledged and submitted to can the power and authority of God's kingdom be made visible in history. God explicitly states that it is His purpose to bring all of history under the rule of Jesus Christ (Ephesians 1:9-10).

Transferring kingdoms can best be illustrated by what happens when a single woman gets married. When she marries, she is transferred from the kingdom of her father to the kingdom of her husband. She is no longer under her father's headship, but under her husband's. The surest way to have problems in a family is for a married woman to go to her father to overrule her husband in her life choices. When that happens, there is inevitably a conflict of kingdoms.

As children of God, we have been transferred from the kingdom of darkness into the kingdom of Jesus Christ. Problems arise when we start listening to our old head, Satan, who owns and runs the kingdom of darkness. This brings us in direct conflict with the kingdom of God.

The second chapter of Colossians gives us an insightful look into the explosive and powerful nature of our union with Christ when we are properly aligned under His kingdom rule.

> See to it that no one takes you captive through hollow and deceptive philosophy, which depends on human tradition and the elemental spiritual forces of this world rather than on Christ. For in Christ all the fullness of the Deity lives in bodily form, and in Christ you have been brought to fullness. *He is the head over every power and authority.* In him you were also circumcised with a circumcision not performed by human hands. Your whole self ruled by the flesh was put off when you were circumcised by Christ, having been buried with him in baptism, in which you were also raised with him through your faith in the working of God, who raised him from the dead (verses 8-12 NIV, emphasis added).

Likewise, we read in Ephesians, "Even when we were dead in our transgressions, [God] made us alive together with Christ (by grace you have been saved), and raised us up with Him, and seated us with Him in the heavenly places in Christ Jesus" (2:5-6).

If you are a believer in Jesus Christ, then when He died, you died with Him. When Christ rose, you rose with Him. When Christ was seated at the right hand of the Father, you were seated with Him. In other words, you were made to function in concert and cadence with Jesus.

In order for you to legitimately access His sovereign authority over all things, you and your world must be aligned under His headship as Lord. This includes your thoughts, choices, words, and perspective. It is in properly aligning yourself under Him and His Word that His authority becomes manifest in your own life as you seek to advance His kingdom on earth.

We can go to all the church services we want, read all the spiritual books we want, and "name and claim" whatever we want, but until we place ourselves under the comprehensive rule of God in every area of our life by aligning ourselves under the lordship of Jesus Christ, we will not fully realize or maximize the rule and authority He has destined for us.

God has appointed a regent—Jesus, who has been elevated above all—to rule over history. Believing in God is not enough to access the authority that comes through Christ. Calling on His names is not enough either. It is the relationship we have to the names of Christ that determines what happens in history, because He has been placed above all rule and authority and—by virtue of who He is—demands first place.

Since Jesus is seated at the right hand of God (the "power side"), His followers are seated there with Him (Ephesians 2:6). You might ask, "But Tony, how can someone be in two places at one time?" Easy, we do it all the time through technology. I can physically be in Dallas, but I can also be in Chicago through Skype. I can be seated in my home and still participate in a board meeting in Atlanta. Through human technology, we can be in two places at once.

Now, if man can produce technology that puts us in two places at one time, then don't you think that the Creator of the universe can do the same thing? You are physically on earth, but you are supposed to be functioning from the position of heaven. You are seated with Christ in the heavenlies. The enemy tries to keep you thinking and functioning from an earthly perspective.

If Satan can keep you thinking that you are bound by the rules of his kingdom rather than accessing the authority of Jesus Christ in the heavenlies, he can keep you perpetually defeated and keep your world broken. The only authority that is the final authority is that of the Lord Jesus Christ. This means you must operate from a divine point of view rather than a human point of view.[5]

Accessing the Lord's Authority

So how do we access this authority that comes wrapped up in how we relate to the Lord? Let's look at a passage Paul wrote in order to reveal our proper relationship to this name and how to activate its authority in our life.

The fullest expression of this name is often given as the Lord Jesus Christ. Jesus is His human name. Christ is His office. Lord is His title. Romans 10:8-13 focuses on His title, which has caused a great deal of confusion for many people.

> "The word is near you, in your mouth and in your heart"—that is, the word of faith which we are preaching, that if you confess with your mouth Jesus as Lord, and believe in your heart that God raised Him from the dead, you will be saved; for with the heart a person believes, resulting in righteousness, and with the mouth he confesses, resulting in salvation. For the Scripture says, "Whoever believes in Him will not be disappointed." For there is no distinction between Jew and Greek; for the same Lord is Lord of all, abounding in riches for all who call on Him; for "Whoever will call on the name of the Lord will be saved."

Let's start off by acknowledging that this passage declares two things that must be done in order for a person to be saved. A person must confess with their mouth and also believe in their heart. According to these verses, then, there appears to be a dual requirement for salvation.

Now, a dual requirement for salvation directly contradicts the other passages in Scripture that only give one requirement to be saved. For example:

• *John 3:16*—"God so loved the world, that He gave

His only begotten Son, that whoever believes in Him shall not perish, but have eternal life."

- *Acts 16:31*—"Believe in the Lord Jesus, and you will be saved, you and your household."

These are just two examples. Over and over in Scripture, we are told that in order to be saved, a person must place their faith in Christ alone for the forgiveness of sins and the gift of eternal life.

Yet in the passage in Romans, there are two things listed: believing and confessing. That leads us to a very important question: Which is right? Must a person do one thing to be saved...or two? What if a person believed in Christ with faith but then had a heart attack before they ever confessed the Lord publicly? Would that person be saved?

The answer to that question is simple once we look at the original language of the passage in Romans. The confusion is found in the word *saved*. For starters, salvation has three tenses to it:

- salvation in the past from the penalty of sin

- salvation in the future from the very presence of sin

- salvation in the present from the power of sin

Even though all three tenses vary greatly in how they apply to a person's life, when this term is interpreted from Greek to English, it is simply translated *saved*. Many people do not realize that the same word can have three different tenses and meanings. But in order to accurately understand a passage in Scripture, the correct definition needs to be conferred. So, when we examine Romans 10:8-13, we have to first determine which tense of the word *saved* is being used. Was Paul writing about being saved from the condemnation of sin, as in accepting Jesus as your personal substitute? Was Paul talking about salvation in heaven, where sin will no longer be a part of the equation? Or was Paul referring to salvation in the present, when the flesh and the devil attempt to affect and worsen our life?

It is in understanding which version of *saved* he is referring to that we will be able to make sense of this passage. In fact, Paul helps us himself in verse 10 when he says, "With the heart a person believes, resulting in righteousness, and with the mouth he confesses, resulting in salvation." According to this verse, a person is made righteous simply by belief.

Thus, when Paul talks about being saved in this passage, he is not talking about going to heaven. In fact, the audience he was writing to were already believers and followers. Rather, in this passage Paul is talking about bringing heaven to you. He is talking about how we as believers can access the daily salvation—or deliverance—we need from the world, the flesh, and the devil.

Let's use baseball as an example of these differences in meaning. In baseball, a pitcher will get credited a "save" when he enters a game with a lead of no more than three runs, and he pitches at least one inning. There are other conditions that must be met and other ways he can get a save, but that is the most common.

Now, a player can be called "safe" when they reach a base

before being tagged by someone with the ball, or—depending on the base and how many runners are on it—before someone with the ball tags the base.

Another way a player can make a nice "save" is when another player commits an error, and this player recovers from the consequences of the error and winds up making the play after all.

There are multiple ways the terms *save* and *safe* can be applied in baseball. Yet, if you were trying to understand this game as someone who doesn't have a familiarity with the English language or the culture, you may be confused and try to apply the various meanings in the wrong situations.

That's one of the problems we run into when we attempt to do a basic, surface-level interpretation of Scripture. A cursory reading of Romans 10:8-13 can quickly confuse our thoughts on how a person gets to heaven. But getting to heaven is not what Paul is talking about here—not even close. The original term set in the original context of what Paul wrote refers more to the third definition given in the baseball illustration. It's about how to get out of a bind or how to get rescued and delivered from a situation you are presently experiencing. This is very different than gaining access into heaven.

In this passage, Paul is not talking about salvation from the past or from the penalty of sin, or even salvation in the future from the presence of sin. He's talking about salvation in the present from the power of sin and the circumstances that result from it.

Thus, if you want to find deliverance and salvation in everyday life and understand how to be an overcomer, you will need to do more than place your faith in Christ. Scripture demands that you get to know the name Lord and confess it (publicly affirm, attest to, and identify with it).

The word *Lord* comes from the Greek word *kurios*, as used in the Septuagint. The Septuagint is the Greek translation of the Old Testament. In the original Hebrew, *kurios* is the word *Yahweh*. Thus, when attached to Jesus, the title is a reference to His deity. When you use the name Lord to refer to Jesus, you are recognizing Him as supreme ruler.

When Thomas doubted Jesus' resurrection but was given visible proof of the risen Jesus in the flesh, he proclaimed, "My Lord and my God!" (John 20:28). Lord is a name that is to inform all we do in life. As Colossians 3:17 says, "Whatever you do in word or deed, do all in the name of the Lord Jesus, giving thanks through Him to God the Father." Friend, you are to declare by your life and by your lips that you are under the rulership of the Lord Jesus. He is over all. Baptism serves as your introduction to your public proclamation. It is the beginning of a lifetime of confession of Jesus as Lord.

Have you ever seen someone who is married but doesn't want to wear their wedding ring? Even though they are legally married, they don't want anyone else to know it. That right there will give you great insight into the quality of that marriage. While we may cringe at the thought of someone doing that to their spouse, God has a lot of members of His family who don't wear His ring by confessing that Jesus is Lord. Sure, they may talk about Him privately or especially in their prayers, but a public acknowledgment—even occasionally— is hard to come by.

There are many reasons why people shy away from declaring Jesus as Lord publicly. One of them is given to us in John 12:42-43:

> Many even of the rulers believed in Him, but because of the Pharisees they were not confessing Him, for fear that they would be put out of the synagogue; for they loved the approval of men rather than the approval of God.

Even though these individuals believed in Jesus as Lord, they feared the consequences of saying so. These verses mention two potential consequences. First was the tangible consequence of being removed from their place of study and worship. Second was the intangible consequence of disapproval from other people. In our culture today, very few—if any—of us face tangible consequences for naming Jesus as Lord. The majority of those who do not regularly confess Jesus as Lord choose not to do so out of fear of the second consequence noted in this passage—the disapproval of people. Yet the failure to confess Jesus as Lord publicly blocks our ability to be delivered (saved) in our everyday life situations. We cannot skip the Lord Jesus and get attention from God. John 5:23 says, "He who does not honor the Son does not honor the Father who sent Him."

The issue of honor and confession has to do with a public association and identification with the Lord Jesus Christ. Confession means that if you were accused of being a follower of Jesus, there would be enough evidence to convict you. You wouldn't be found innocent of all charges.

Most Christians are not aware of how seriously this impacts their lives. If they were, we would see and hear a lot more people confessing Jesus as Lord publicly. But in Matthew 10:33, it couldn't be plainer: "Whoever denies Me before men, I will also deny him before My Father who is in heaven." That is pretty straightforward. Deny Jesus publicly, and He will do the same for you when you are seeking intervention in prayer from God above. But the previous verse tells us how we can open up that flow of favor and help. "Everyone who confesses Me before men, I will also confess him before My Father who is in heaven" (verse 32).

These two verses are so critical to understanding how we can live out the victorious Christian life that we would be wise to write them on a tablet and wear it around our neck as a reminder. This *is* the key. Revelation 12:11 tells us, "They overcame [the accuser] because of the blood of the Lamb and because of the word of their testimony." The word of their testimony gave them access to the power that the blood of the Lamb had secured for them.

Friend, if you are ashamed of any public association with Jesus as Lord, then you are sabotaging your own spiritual pathway to living your destiny. One of the reasons we have so little deliverance among the body of believers today is because we have so little public confession of Jesus as Lord accompanied by a submission to His authority—which is what calling on someone as Lord implies. Sure, we have plenty of crosses hanging around our neck, on the walls of our home, or in our church. But Jesus as Lord of our life means more than that. It means He rules. He chooses. His viewpoint is the viewpoint we go by. What He says and what He does ought to inform what we say and what we do entirely. There is no area of your life that He cannot speak into and should not speak into. There is no area of your finances, relationships, attitudes, work, or anything else that He cannot overrule.

Jesus in not a decoration. He is not a logo or an icon. He is not a brand. He is Lord. Ruler. Master. King. The authority over all (Ephesians 1:22). Until this lordship question is settled both in and through you publicly, heaven's help will remain a long way away. His divine presence, intervention, transformation, deliverance, healing, and guidance will elude you simply because you do not comply in this area of confession.

For far too many Christians, Jesus is prominent—He's just not preeminent. He's popular—He's just not primary. He gets some of your attention as you attend church, say grace before you eat, read a Bible verse in the morning, or add some decorations on your shelf. But when it comes to choosing between Jesus (what He says, where He guides, what He requires) and your other affections in life (personal, emotional, physical, friends, media, etc.), Jesus usually loses.

But ultimately, you lose.

You lose because Jesus *is* your access to all you need in order to live your life according to the maximum expression and power you can have.

Calling on the Lord

As we've seen throughout this book and the various passages we've studied together, there is nothing that sits outside Jesus our Lord. Remember Colossians 1:15-18, which says:

> He is the image of the invisible God, the first-
> born of all creation. For by Him all things were
> created, both in the heavens and on earth, visi-
> ble and invisible, whether thrones or dominions
> or rulers or authorities—all things have been cre-
> ated through Him and for Him. He is before all
> things, and in Him all things hold together. He
> is also head of the body, the church; and He is
> the beginning, the firstborn from the dead, so
> that He Himself will come to have first place in
> everything.

There exists no subject, education, business, accomplish-
ment, ministry, home, or anything else in the hands of a Christian from which Jesus should be excluded. He is the all in all.
Yet when things are going well, we have a tendency to forget that. We have a tendency to believe our own press. Until,
that is, things start to go left. When that business, relationship, health, or home starts to veer left, we call on Him right
quick. Don't we?

What Jesus wants to know when you call on Him in times
of need is whether or not you confessed Him publicly when
times were good. Since everything is attached to Him, your
confession shows up in what you say, the decisions you make,
the reasons you make them, what you think, what you pursue,
and more. It all must align under and be informed by Jesus
your Lord. And while you will never carry out this part of the
Christian life perfectly—after all, you are human and prone to
whims of selfishness—you must seek to do it better progres-
sively. You must apply yourself to growing in the knowledge

of the lordship of Jesus Christ. All of life is to be lived in recognition of the lordship of Jesus (Romans 14:8-9).

Philippians 2 tells us we will all reach that day when we confess Jesus as Lord. Whether you do so now or not is up to you, but everyone *will* do so.

> God highly exalted Him, and bestowed on Him the name which is above every name, so that at the name of Jesus every knee will bow, of those who are in heaven and on earth and under the earth, and that every tongue will confess that Jesus Christ is Lord, to the glory of God the Father (verses 9-11).

God doesn't just want you to confess Jesus. He doesn't just want you to confess Jesus Christ. He desires for you to confess Jesus as Lord. Why? Because it brings Him glory. When you recognize the lordship of Jesus Christ, that He is above all, you bring glory to God. But to deny the lordship, rulership, and ownership of Jesus is to dishonor God. It is to erect a roadblock between yourself and the answers to your prayers for heaven's intervention, deliverance, and salvation on earth. Public identification with and submission to the lordship of Jesus Christ gives a believer the legal right to call on the name of the Lord for divine assistance and deliverance (i.e., to be saved; Romans 5:9-10; 10:9,13). Calling on the name of the Lord is a specifically Christian action and privilege (1 Corinthians 1:2; 2 Timothy 2:22; Acts 7:59).

Friend, Jesus is over all. He is over you. He is over me. To the degree that we seek to make this reality known to a lost and dying world is the degree to which we experience the full manifestation of His power in our daily lives.

There is a story told about an indigenous boy who was about to be mauled by a lion. The lion had leapt at him and got his paws on him. But there was a man in the area who had learned how to defeat a lion. He quickly grabbed some wire and jumped on the lion's back. When the man wrapped the wire around the lion's throat, the lion's attention turned from the boy to the pain it was experiencing. The boy quickly ran off while the man wrestled with the lion long enough to make his own escape as well.

A few weeks later, the man who had saved the boy's life heard some rumblings outside his home. When he looked outside, he saw the young boy walking up to his door, carrying a large amount of belongings. Behind the boy marched a number of other people carrying more of his belongings to help him. The man asked the boy what he was doing. The boy calmly replied, "You saved my life. And in my tribe, when someone saves your life, they own you. I am in your service for the rest of my life."

It's a fictional story, but it paints a picture with which we can identify. After all, without Jesus exercising His authority over all rule and all power as Lord, we would not have the opportunity to pass from death to life into eternity. If you are a born-again believer, Jesus has saved your life. Yet not only does He save it for eternity, but He also offers to save your life each and every moment you call on Him in His name while publicly confessing His lordship over you.

Knowing all of that is true, it should be no issue to give

Jesus your life and your service willingly for the remainder of your time on earth. If anyone has a problem with that or makes you feel uncomfortable for your public confession of Jesus as Lord, just remember that no one else died in order to deliver you from a sentence of certain eternal death. They didn't get you to heaven. The Lord Jesus Christ did that. And it is that same power that can bring heaven's intervention into your life right now. Make a commitment that from this moment forward, you will seek to publicly confess the name of Jesus as Lord in all you think, do, say, and decide. Then watch heaven pour out its unending power on you.

She will bear a Son; and you shall call His name Jesus, for He will save His people from their sins.

MATTHEW 1:21

But you were washed, but you were sanctified, but you were justified in the name of the Lord Jesus Christ and in the Spirit of our God.

1 CORINTHIANS 6:11

9

JESUS

John. James. Robert. Michael. These are some of the most common boy names in America. You have probably met someone by one of these names—if not all. For whatever reason, parents frequently choose to name their sons these names. It could be due to their meanings. It might have to do with the names of relatives or ancestors. Whatever the case, these names tend to get passed down more often than most.

Just like the name Jesus.

Not so much today, that is. But at the time Jesus was born more than 2,000 years ago, Jesus was a common name. In our modern context, many probably can't imagine naming a child Jesus. There is too much identity wrapped up in the name. But at the time of His birth, it was a name that evoked little thought or attribution. It carries a significant meaning but, most likely, that meaning was rarely thought of by those giving the name. Except in the case of Jesus, our Christ.

Jesus was not named by His parents. This specific name was not given to Him by His human mother or father. We discover in Scripture's account of His birth that heaven sent a message to Joseph through an angel and told him what to name Jesus. Jesus was not Joseph's biological child, but He was the child Joseph would help raise. Thus, the message of what to call Him came to the earthly father from His true heavenly Father. God instructed Joseph to name the baby Jesus (see Matthew 1:18-25).

This common name would grow to eventually become His most well-known name. Jesus means "Savior," "rescuer," and "deliverer." The Old Testament name for Jesus was Joshua.

If you'll recall, Joshua was the man who delivered the Israelites into the promised land. He was fierce and full of faith. He led the Israelites in such a way as to overcome the enemies in the land. The name Joshua (and its corresponding Greek name, Jesus) refers to a person who leads the way into a place of blessing—a person who delivers people from their enemies.

Thus, God chose a name for His only-begotten Son that means "Savior." The primary identity reflected in Jesus' name is that of someone who came to deliver people from something over which they needed victory. Jesus came to rescue each one of us. Matthew 1:21 says it clearly: "She will bear a Son; and you shall call His name Jesus, for He will save His people from their sins." The word *save* here can also be translated as *rescue*.

Jesus' Main Mission

First and foremost, Jesus came to rescue us from our sins. When I was a water safety instructor and lifeguard, my primary role was to rescue people from drowning. Sure, I had other roles like teaching people how to swim, offering guidance on ways to swim better, and providing a support system for the people visiting the pool. But all of that was secondary to my primary goal: to save lives should anyone be at risk of drowning. Had I not been able to fulfill this primary goal, I would not have been a lifeguard. Saving lives was the central nature of my job description.

The reason I'm emphasizing this idea of a foundational role is because people often want to use Jesus for everything else other than His primary role. They want Jesus to rescue them from poor health, debt, relationship issues, emotional issues, and more. And while Jesus is sufficient to come to our aid in all these things—as we have seen in other chapters—if we do not look to Him first as the one who rescues us from our sins, we bypass the foundation upon which all else rests.

The central mission of Jesus is that of saving us from our sins. We read in John 3:36, "He who believes in the Son has eternal life; but he who does not obey the Son will not see life, but the wrath of God abides on him."

He came to save us and give us eternal life, but He also came that we might fully experience that life in the present (John 10:10). This is something we could only do after Jesus abolished the wrath of God for us through His substitutionary atonement.

One of the reasons Jesus does not come through for us in ways we wish He would in other areas of life is because we often skip the sin issue and go straight to what we want. We skip our acknowledgment of the primary reason why He came and try to use Him like a vending machine instead. But Jesus came first and foremost to deal with our sins—both saving us for eternity through His atonement and saving us on earth through His ongoing intercession, supplying us power to resist and overcome temptation and the continual consequences of sin (Hebrews 7:25).

When we want Jesus to rescue us from the peripheral rather than the central issue at hand, even when the peripheral is important, we miss out on His approach and strategy for rescuing us from it all. When we do not allow Him to deal with the central issue in our life (sin), then we cannot call on Him for all the other things, because all the other things we wrestle with are rooted in sin.

Everything negative in your life is related either directly or indirectly to the presence of sin. You are either experiencing the consequences of your own sin or someone else's, or your issue arises from a contaminated, sinful environment—one in which we all live, work, and play. The latter includes those things that exist because evil has invaded the atmosphere, affecting us emotionally, circumstantially, relationally, socially, physically, as well as spiritually. Similar to how the flu invades the atmosphere in which we live and breathe, sin surrounds us as we live in this contaminated environment.

But who wants to talk about sin? Other than charismatic preachers and tent revivalists, most people consider sin a taboo subject today. Bible studies rarely, if ever, focus on sin. Sermon series don't either. Personal devotional time is often geared toward ways in which to be encouraged by Jesus' presence and purpose, not on how to acknowledge and then rid ourselves of sin. In fact, instead of calling out sin for what it is, we often downplay it in the words we use. We might call it "a mistake" or say, "It's just my personality." Sometimes we label sin an "issue."

In our self-promoting contemporary culture, sin just doesn't sit well in most of our conversations.

Yet if Jesus cannot deal with this main issue in our lives, then everything else we face will only continue to pile up until it eventually runs over the banks of our circumstances and floods us.

We might gain a better appreciation for the person of Jesus as our Savior if we look more closely at the nature of God. For starters, God lives in His perfect state of being. Everything about Him is perfect. He is flawless. He has no issues and makes no mistakes. God views sin as sin. All sin evokes His response because He is pure. For example, if you were to go into an operating room with a handful of dirt and put it on the patient, that person would then be contaminated. But even if you were to go in and put tiny bacteria on a scalpel that is used during the surgery—even if you can't see the bacteria—contamination would still take place.

See, in an operating room, everything has to be sterilized. The doctors and nurses have to wash their hands and follow a protocol of cleanliness in order to protect the patient from even the slightest contamination. Because even the slightest contamination can lead to disastrous results.

God is "sterilized." Everything about Him is perfect, and He cannot and will not allow even the slightest contamination to enter His presence. Therefore, the issue of sin is an enormous one, and God set up the protocol for addressing it through His Son, Jesus. Addressing sin sits as the foundation of all we can do in our lives. If we don't address it the way God has prescribed, we block our access to His presence and power. It's kind of like trying to treat cancer with over-the-counter medicine. It won't work. Jesus came so that we might have a way to repair the root of our problems. And until we allow Him to get to the root, our attempts at reversing the symptoms of sin will be temporary at best. We might mask the symptoms and consequences for a few hours. But when that distraction wears off or that 12-step program runs dry, we won't completely heal from the deep wound all sin creates in our life.

In Mark 2 we read about a time when some friends brought a paralyzed man to Jesus for healing. But Jesus didn't start out by healing the man's physical issues. Rather, He began by telling the man that his sins were forgiven (verse 5). While the man and his friends sought a physical cure, Jesus knew a spiritual cure was of greater importance. That's what Jesus addressed first. He wanted to get the man back in spiritual alignment with God before He addressed the physical.

It's like when a child falls off a bike and skins their knee. The parent doesn't automatically apply medication to the open wound in order to promote healing. No, first they have to wash the dirt off the wound and possibly even pick out gravel. Any amount of dirt or gravel, no matter how tiny it is, will only give rise to even larger physical issues down the road. A cleansing must occur before the salve can fully work to produce healing.

Jesus is God's representative to deal with the mire and muck

of our sin. It is through the cleansing power of His blood that
we discover the cure to anything and everything that seeks to
tear us down. See, the devil has a goal. Sin is not some arbi-
trary, floating mass of germs just waiting for a host. No, Satan
tempts us to sin, and he has a distinct goal: death (John 10:10).
Satan has come to steal and kill, and he knows that the cost of
sin is death (Romans 6:23)—whether it's physical death, relational separation, or emotional death, it doesn't matter to him.

As I mentioned, death can be applied in many ways. But
ultimately it signifies a division or separation from what was
once good. Death in the Bible most often refers to a separation,
not a cessation. For example, when a person dies—whether
that person goes to heaven or hell—they haven't stopped living. It's just that the spirit and soul have left the body, and the
body is no longer able to function. Thus, the goal of sin is to
bring about a separation. Always. It might mean a separation
from God as our fellowship becomes tarnished. Or it could
mean a separation from one another. Whether it's a racial crisis
or a social crisis, widespread sin separates the unity in humanity that God desires us to have.

Far too often we get hung up on the physical aspects and
tangible realities of life and neglect to address the sin. In the
case of racism, for example, we wind up talking about skin
and not sin. We wind up with centuries of confusion in our
nation because we have failed to address the root of the problem, which is how we sin when we view others as less than
us. And as long as the conversation focuses on the social—or
the economic, political, relational, or even personal—instead
of the spiritual, we will be stuck looking at how to fix the

symptoms rather than how to kill the root. I'm sure you know what happens to weeds when you fail to address the root. They resprout and spread after you trim them, usually with an even greater vengeance.

Friend, you can save a lot of time when dealing with issues in your life, home, work, or community if you start with the sin issue. Deal with the root, and the rest will adjust. Jesus did not come only to fix symptoms. He came to fix causes, which then results in repaired symptoms. Unless you deal with the cause of the problem at hand, you will forever be dealing with patchwork approaches. Your situation may get better for a while, but the problem will reappear.

Kinds of Sin

Just like a variety of bacteria exists in the world, sin doesn't come in a one-size-fits-all neatly packaged container. We all have sinned, yes. But these sins are as varied as the snowflakes in a storm. Whether it is a sin of commission (something a person does purposefully) or a sin of omission (sin resulting from not doing what you should; James 4:17), all sin results in death.

Not only is there a multitude of manners in which people sin, but there are also three distinct categories of sin: imputed, inherited, and personal.

Imputed Sin

The word *imputed* means "credited to someone's account." If your employer offers an automatic deposit for your paycheck, you don't receive cash on payday. Nor do you receive a check. What you receive is known as credit. By receiving that credit, you now have the ability to access those funds, even though no tangible money ever changed hands when you got paid.

In Romans 5:12, we come across our imputed sin: "Just as through one man sin entered into the world, and death through sin, and so death spread to all men, because all sinned." The human race received a death credit because of Adam's sin. What Adam did carried over to all of us. Through his wrongdoing, we inherited our sin nature and the consequence of his sin, which is death.

You might not think this sounds too fair. Let me use my favorite sport, football, to help illustrate the point. When a lineman jumps offside before a play, he isn't the only one penalized. Because the team plays as a team, scores as a team, and defends as a team, the lineman's penalty becomes the team's penalty. Essentially, the sin of the lineman is imputed to the other members of his team, even though none of them jumped offside. Why? Because they are connected.

The Bible declares that we are all connected to the human race through Adam. And because Adam sinned, then the whole human race was credited with the consequence of that sin and thus penalized with death. The substitutionary death of Christ solved the problem of imputed sin, which is why infants and those who do not have a mental capacity to understand sin are covered (Romans 5:17-19).

Inherited Sin

Inherited sin is what each of us receives from our parents and ancestors. It's also what we pass on to our own children. We know this as our "sin nature." Every person ever born (outside of Jesus) has a sin nature. It's in the DNA due to the introduction of sin by Adam. Thus, when you have children yourself, you not only give them your good looks, but you also give them your propensity to sin. That's why a parent never has to teach a child how to be selfish, how to be sneaky, or how to lie. What a parent has to teach a child is how to share, how to love, and how to be patient.

Sin is inherited. We all face it. We all struggle with it. We all must seek to overcome it. And while some of us are better at managing our sin nature than others, we all have a sin nature to contend with. Whether it shows up outwardly in obvious words or actions, or whether it is a selfish, proud spirit that is known only between you and God, a sin nature produces sin, which then produces death (Romans 6:23).

Personal Sin

Let's forget Adam for a moment. Let's forget your parents and ancestors for a time. Let's just look at you and me. Because personal sin is the sin we know we shouldn't do, but we go ahead and do it anyway. Or it is the right action we know we should take, but we choose not to out of a heart of apathy or selfishness.

We all sin in this way. Some of us may let others see it more than the next person, but God doesn't look at humanity like we do. God looks at the heart (1 Samuel 16:7). He sees our heart even better than we do. After all, our heart deceives us more than we often realize (Jeremiah 17:9). To "follow your heart" is usually not a wise thing to do because your heart is tainted with sin's influence.

Whether personal sin shows up boldly or lurks behind a veil of secrecy, God knows it is there. Sin can never be hidden; it can only be forgiven. And when it is not repented from through a heart seeking forgiveness, then it brings about death. That's just what sin does. The wages of sin is always death. There is nowhere we can run from the complications that sin produces in our life. While we may think we can escape from one consequence, we cannot. Consequences show up everywhere, whether in emotional death, relational death, financial death, or eternal death. Sin breeds separation. It gives birth to a disquieting distance in families, among races, in churches, and in our own thoughts and personal lives—giving rise to chaos, emptiness, loss, and atrophy.

In Jesus' Name

But there is good news in this "bad news" chapter. The good news is that Jesus came so we would never have to die. In any and every category of death we can experience, when our faith is placed in Christ alone for the forgiveness of our sin, He restores life. As John 11:26 says, "Everyone who lives and believes in Me will never die."

We also read in 2 Corinthians 5:8, "We are of good courage, I say, and prefer rather to be absent from the body and to be at home with the Lord." Physical death is only absence from the body. It does not equate to spiritual death or separation from God when a person is saved by Jesus Christ. In fact, when you die physically, you won't be dead long enough to know that you died. You will immediately be transferred to the heavenly realm and into the presence of the Lord (see Luke 23:43).

The reason that you should never fear death is because Jesus soundly dealt with the penalty of sin so that physical death, for a believer, is merely a momentary transition. Jesus has rescued us from the power of sin.

And while His salvation secures our eternal destiny when we believe in Him and His promise of eternal life, He also saves us from the power of sin and its ability to mess up our lives here on earth. He does both. Far too many of us deal with things related to our emotions, finances, relationships, and more that have come about due to our sin. But when we approach God from the wrong perspective, we fail to get the help we need. For example, some people go to God because their credit card debt has piled too high, and they say, "God, help me pay my bills." But God always deals with the root first—the sin that caused the debt. His response may be, "You sinned in the area of your money." And if they don't want to deal with that sin—to repent (admit what they did wrong and turn away from continuing it)—then He won't just skip over the sin to pay their bills.

Jesus brings life and deliverance, but He does it His way. He died for your sin—both the future and present effects. But there is a pathway to that deliverance that we cannot skip if we hope to obtain it. Second Corinthians 5:21 says, "He made Him who knew no sin to be sin on our behalf, *so that* we might become the righteousness of God in Him" (emphasis added).

So that. Those are two short, monosyllabic words, but they carry the key to our victory in Jesus. He became sin on our behalf *so that* we might become the righteousness of God. Only when we seek His forgiveness and atonement by repenting of our sins do we experience this righteousness He gives. Only He can overcome whatever issue it is you are facing, but you tap into that overcoming power by being transformed through His forgiveness. Romans 5:10 says, "If while we were enemies we were reconciled to God through the death of His Son, much more, having been reconciled, we shall be saved by His life." Jesus lives in order to rescue you from the effects of sin. That is why He came.

One of the most powerful passages in Scripture is often attributed only to physical death, but it means so much more.

> Behold, I tell you a mystery; we will not all sleep, but we will all be changed, in a moment, in the twinkling of an eye, at the last trumpet; for the trumpet will sound, and the dead will be raised imperishable, and we will be changed. For this perishable must put on the imperishable, and this mortal must put on immortality. But when this perishable will have put on the imperishable, and this mortal will have put on immortality, then will come about the saying that is written, "Death is swallowed up in victory. O death, where is your victory? O death, where is your sting?" The sting of death is sin, and the power of sin is the law; but thanks be to God, who gives us the victory through our Lord Jesus Christ (1 Corinthians 15:51-57).

In this deeply touching section of Scripture, one in which countless souls have found refuge and solace, Paul declares Jesus' victory over death. But it is not only physical death over which He has waged warfare and won. Jesus holds the victory over any death-dealing blow you face. Because He lives, you can overcome anything and everything sin throws your way. And you gain access to His life through His name. But what most people fail to grasp is that victory doesn't come merely through a recitation of or an appeal to His name; it is also based on our relationship to His name.

You cannot just say "Jesus" and get heaven's intervention in your situation on earth—even though preachers may preach that message and congregations may shout His name boldly, repeating it for effect. Most of us end our prayers by saying, "In Jesus' name," because that's what we have been taught to pray. And while that is important to do, unless there exists an open flow between us and Jesus made possible through forgiveness, we don't have the rightful and legal use of His name.

Let me illustrate it this way. When a person has power of attorney, that means someone else has given them permission to use their name in their place. They have been given legal permission from another person to act on their behalf. Without the official designation of power of attorney, someone else cannot choose what is done on behalf of another person's property or finances. I think we can all understand this because it is an established process set up by our court system. But what few of us understand when it comes to Jesus' name is that unless we have been given legitimate permission to use His name through the process of forgiveness and abiding in Him, then we have not been granted "power of attorney" to use His name with authority.

See, Jesus' name is not a magical term like "hocus pocus."

It doesn't come infused with superhero powers. Rather, Jesus' name gives you access to a power greater than any magic or superhero powers could ever be—when it is used in conjunction with a right relationship to Him.

In Acts 19, we see a perfect example of this. Because Paul had traveled around various towns casting out demons in Jesus' name, other people began to see this as a profit-producing business. They thought the secret sauce was Jesus' name, so they proceeded to use it. However, when they went to cast out a demon, the demon told them point blank that while it had heard of Paul and knew Jesus, it did not know them. The demon-possessed man then proceeded to jump on them, overcome them, strip them naked, and wound them (verses 11-16).

These individuals desired to get rid of demons. They employed a strategy they had seen work. But when they went to make the demon leave, it attacked them instead and chased them off.

In other words, just because they knew the name Jesus and used it did not mean they had legitimate right to access the authority found in the name. This truth applies to all of us as well. That's why 1 John 5:14-15 says, "This is the confidence which we have before Him, that, if we ask anything according to His will, He hears us. And if we know that He hears us in whatever we ask, we know that we have the requests which we have asked from Him." The caveat we find here is the clause "according to His will." God is not going to respond to your use of Jesus' name if you are not equally concerned with doing His will. Anything apart from His will is disobedience since He sits over all and rules over all. And one of the foundational principles of His will is that sin must be dealt with first—for-given through the atonement of Jesus in order that realignment in obedience can take place. Using Jesus' name without His authorization leaves Him with no obligation to respond.

Friend, if you are going to end your prayers "in Jesus' name," make sure that you are first letting God identify your sin in order for you to repent and receive His offer of forgiveness for your sin. Forgiveness frees Him up to address the circumstances and deliverance for which you just prayed. But if you choose to skip His will, you've just wasted your time with a tagline.

John 15:7 says, "If you abide in Me, and My words abide in you, ask whatever you wish, and it will be done for you." John 14:13-15 emphasizes this as well: "Whatever you ask in My name, that will I do, so that the Father may be glorified in the Son. If you ask Me anything in My name, I will do it. If you love Me, you will keep My commandments."

Loving Jesus means keeping His commandments. Abiding in Jesus means having the truth of His Word—His viewpoint on every decision you make—govern you. When these two things take place, you are guaranteed His deliverance. You are guaranteed to receive whatever you ask. Because when you do these two things, you are in His will, and whatever it is you are asking, He desires as well.

The power of Jesus' name has the ability to free you for all eternity, but His name also has the authority to give you victory in every situation you face right now.

Jesus may have been a common name in the cultural context into which Jesus was born. But because of what He did and who He is, this name has never been the same since. And it will never be the same in the future either. In fact, in the future, every knee will bow to this name and every tongue will confess this name—no matter how powerful the person is or how large their influence in heaven or on earth (Philippians 2:9-11).

I don't know who the so-called "powerful" people are in your life. I don't know the name you might throw around when you are nonchalantly name dropping. It could be a celebrity's name. It could be a doctor's name. It could be an athlete's name. But no matter how great that name might be right now, and no matter how many doors get opened when you mention you know that person, there is no other name as strong and powerful as Jesus. And when you choose to abide in Him and allow His Word to abide in you, obeying Him as best you can and seeking forgiveness for when you don't, you will discover that this name opens doors no one could have ever opened for you. It also closes doors that Satan intends to harm you or to keep you from living out your purpose and destiny.

When you get this name right and rightly align yourself under Jesus, you will get to see heaven visit earth, addressing sin and changing circumstances. Remember, God sent Jesus to address sin—not to make you comfortable in it.

*Was it not necessary for the Christ to suffer
these things and to enter into His glory? Then
beginning with Moses and with all the prophets,
He explained to them the things concerning
Himself in all the Scriptures.*

LUKE 24:26-27

*More than that, I count all things to be loss in
view of the surpassing value of knowing Christ
Jesus my Lord, for whom I have suffered the loss
of all things, and count them but rubbish so
that I may gain Christ.*

PHILIPPIANS 3:8

10

CHRIST

M y given name is Anthony Tyrone Evans. That's the name my parents chose for me when I was born. Most people, though, know my name as Tony Evans. When I hear that name, I turn around to respond because that is who I identify as. Now, when I'm with my family at home, I will also identify as Poppy (from the grandkids), Daddy (from the kids), and Tony or Doc (from my wife). If I am gathered with family and someone says "Anthony," I'm going to keep doing what I'm doing and not look up, because that is the name my son goes by.

On the premises where I work with our national ministry, or when I am on the road speaking, people will add the title doctor before my name due to my earned doctorate in theology. Thus, I most often hear others say "Dr. Evans" in meetings or when traveling and speaking as a guest.

On the church grounds where I serve as senior pastor,

people don't normally call me Anthony, Tony, Tony Evans, or even Dr. Evans. At church, I am consistently called Pastor. When I hear someone say "Pastor" there, I will turn to look because the person is most likely referring to me. If any of the associate pastors are being addressed, congregants or staff will typically add their last name, such as Pastor Gibson, or substitute a nickname, like Pastor G. In this way, it is easy for me and others to identify whom people are speaking to when only "Pastor" is said.

When I get emails or letters from listeners of my broadcast, they will often use a combination of these names, such as Dr. Tony Evans, pastor. Essentially, they put my personal name with my title and add my role in one form of expression.

As you can see, there are a great many ways people can refer to one person. They can separate out names, like Tony, Doc, or Pastor. Or they can combine names, like Dr. Tony Evans, based on the relationship and setting. Whether my names come packaged together or are separated in their use, people are still talking about me when they use any of my names.

Let's carry over these thoughts to the names of Jesus. We find a variety of names by which Jesus is called throughout Scripture. When the names King of kings and Lord of lords are packaged together, He is known as the Lord Jesus Christ. At times we just read about Jesus. At other times, He's simply known as Lord or Christ. While all the writers who referenced Him were speaking about the same person, there exists unique nuances to each of His names.

I hope that in giving you a contemporary comparison, you are beginning to see how the various names of Jesus are not random. They have intentionality and meaning. For example, Tony Evans is my personal identity. Doctor is my title. Pastor is my role or responsibility. Poppy signifies my relationship with my grandchildren. Likewise, Jesus is our Lord's personal identity. The meaning of that name is "Savior" and "deliverer," as we saw in the last chapter. Jesus' personal name references His purpose and ability to rescue and deliver us—predominantly from sin, but He also spent three years of His ministry delivering people out of difficult circumstances as well, such as demonic oppression, lameness, blindness, and hunger. Jesus is in the rescuing business, which is consistent with His name.

In addition to the name Jesus, we also know Him as Christ. Now, Christ is not Jesus' last name. It is His role or office. The word *Christ* is the Greek translation of the Hebrew word *Messiah*. That's why it says in John 1:41, "[Andrew] found first his own brother Simon and said to him, 'We have found the Messiah' (which translated means Christ)." Thus, when you see the word *Christ*—a name used more than 500 times in the New Testament—you are reading the Old Testament word *Messiah*.

To understand *Christ*, then, we first have to understand *Messiah*. The word *Messiah* literally means "the anointed one." It refers to the chosen one, called for a specific purpose and given the power to carry out that purpose from God Himself. The name Christ reflects the role of being chosen and empowered by God for His unique anointed purpose.

When Andrew said they had found the Messiah in John 1:41, he was talking about someone he had been looking for. We know this by Andrew's use of the word *found*. If a person says they have found something, implied within that statement is that they were looking for something. In fact, it wasn't only Andrew who had been looking for the anointed one. It was all of Israel. The entire Old Testament was written in anticipation of the one to come who would fulfill the role of Messiah. This is known as the messianic hope. It is impossible to fully understand the Old Testament unless you also understand the messianic hope. Generation after generation after generation after generation looked forward to this promised person of God who would come not only for the Israelites, but who would come to impact the entire world through the establishment of the kingdom of God on earth. The person they looked for was the Messiah, known in Greek (the language of the New Testament) as the Christ.

Luke 24:25-27 gives us the culmination of that long walk on the Emmaus road, when Jesus spent time with a couple of His downtrodden followers after His death and resurrection (although they did not immediately recognize Him). It is in these verses that we see Jesus revisiting the Old Testament to explain who He was. These followers were discouraged, after all, because they had expected Him to deliver Israel from Roman oppression (verse 21), but instead they had witnessed His death, not anticipating His resurrection. So as Jesus walked with them, He returned to the Old Testament to reveal who He was. In doing so, He referenced the Christ.

> He said to them, "O foolish men and slow of heart
> to believe in all that the prophets have spoken!
> Was it not necessary for the Christ to suffer these
> things and to enter into His glory?" Then begin-
> ning with Moses and with all the prophets, He

explained to them the things concerning Himself in all the Scriptures (verses 25-27).

The whole Old Testament, while not using Jesus' personal
name, anticipates Jesus' person coming as the Messiah (or
Christ). For example, in Genesis 3:15, we read that the woman
would have a "seed" through which would come this Messiah.
Now, whenever we talk about the seed for a baby, we are refer-
encing the sperm provided by a man. Yet, in this case it is written that the woman has the seed. This is because there would
be no man involved in creating a child born to a virgin. The
Messiah would come through the seed of a woman, which
would connect with the Spirit of God Himself.

Genesis 3:15 is our introduction to the one who would
come to fulfill the role of the anointed one. As we move on
through the Old Testament, we see how God set up an entire
system of sacrifices in anticipation of the coming Messiah. He
set up a whole festival arrangement looking toward the arrival
of the Messiah. He even made certain promises to Israel—and
through Israel, to the whole world—that would be fulfilled by
the reign of the Messiah.

We also run across a number of prayers in the Bible that
look forward to the coming of the Messiah. We read sermons
about how justice would rule at the coming of the Messiah.
The central message of the Old Testament revolves around
anticipating the one who was to come and embody the messianic hope.

Thus, in the context of how the Israelites understood the
Messiah and His role, when Andrew said they had "found
the Messiah" (John 1:41), he was saying they had found the

one about whom the entire Old Testament had prophesied and spoken. Jesus is the Christ, the anointed one from God who fulfills the promises put forth by God for the world.

The Lineage of Christ

We have briefly looked at the lineage of Jesus in an earlier chapter, but it bears repeating due to its relevancy to this specific name. Scripture says the Christ, the anointed one, was to come through the lineage of King David.

Now, I know that reading names and genealogies in the Bible is probably not your favorite thing to do—nor is it mine. When we come upon a passage about someone who begat someone else, who then begat someone else, etc., it can become a bit boring. Yet this portion of Scripture we are about to discuss is absolutely critical reading, even if it does strike us as boring. The reason why I say it is critical is because of how it relates to prophecy.

In AD 70, after the Jews' rejection of Christ, the Roman general Titus destroyed the Jewish temple, as well as the city of Jerusalem. In this widespread destruction, the genealogical records for the Jews were lost. To put the importance of this in contemporary context, it might have been similar to how we can go to a records building or access software programs today to find out historical information. In one act of prideful power, all those Jewish records were destroyed. All the records except for one, that is.

The record of Jesus' lineage was preserved for us in the writings of Matthew and Luke. And through the preservation of this history, we discover that when God connected Mary and

Joseph, He connected two people who both descended from David.

In Matthew 1, we read that Jesus came through the legal line of David. And in Luke 3, we read that He also came through the biological line of David. This then satisfied the Old Testament prophecy that the Messiah would come through the Davidic line. This reminds us that God knows how to bring two people together in order to fulfill His kingdom purposes. He is always intentional.

When Andrew said they had found the anointed one (John 1:41), he was referring to the anointed one who had come through the line of David. Now, in Scripture, to receive an anointing was to be elected to an office and empowered for that office. In today's culture, you could consider it akin to having an election where candidates run for an office. When someone is elected to an office, they would be considered as having the "anointing" in Old Testament culture.

In biblical days, there were three distinct offices to which someone could be "elected." One classification of an anointed person in the Old Testament was a prophet. The prophet was someone who had been chosen by God to speak on His behalf. This is why a prophet would begin what they had to say with these words (or something similar): "Thus says the Lord." Not only did a prophet speak on behalf of God, but they also foretold the future. Their words were often predictive in nature. They would pass on what God had said, which would frequently include a declaration of events that had not yet happened.

A second classification of those anointed in the Old

Testament was a priest. We already looked at this office more fully in chapter 5, but let's have a refresher here because it is so critical.

In Jewish culture, there existed an entire line of priests. This line of priests would be anointed for the express purpose of acting as mediators between God and humanity. Because humanity is sinful, people could not go directly to God. Due to God's holiness, He would not come close to the sinfulness of people. To bridge this gap, God established a mediator known as a priest. This person would stand between God and the people through sacrificing for the forgiveness of sins.

As a result of these sacrifices, God would then have fellowship with the people and bring blessing upon them. But the priest had to follow a specific plan to carry out his role. If the priest deviated from that plan (for example, by touching the ark irreverently or breaking any of the commands for entering God's presence), the priest would die. When it comes to holiness and sin, God doesn't mess around. That's why He provided a mediator who had to mediate according to specific rules.

Now, among the priests there would be one known as the chief priest. He could also be called the high priest. This high priest would go into a place known as the Holy of Holies once a year to offer sacrifices for the entire nation of Israel. He had to follow certain processes in order to do so, and no one else could enter that area of the temple or they would die. As you might imagine, the priesthood was an anointed role that others did not try to fulfill themselves.

A third classification of anointing was that of a king. The

king was anointed by God for his role in civil responsibilities and ruling over the nation. When the king was chosen, he would go through an official anointing ceremony, which would declare him as the elected one under God who would rule over the nation. The king was either blessed by God or experienced consequences from God for the way he carried out his anointed role.

These three classifications of anointing—that of prophet, priest, and king—were each to be fulfilled in one role at a future date through the Messiah. This unique messianic role would combine all three positions into one. That's why at Christ's baptism, as recorded in Matthew 3:16, the heavens opened up and He experienced the anointing of the Holy Spirit. This anointing launched Jesus into His trifold ministry as prophet, priest, and king.

Learning this context for Christ's name helps inform you as you read and study the Scriptures. Why? Because every time you hear or read the name Christ, you should also think of the name Messiah. And every time you hear or read the name Messiah, you should also think of the name Christ. For both of these names, you should also think of the term *anointed one* and how that references three distinctly elected roles or offices—those of prophet, priest, and king.

Christ embodies all three of these anointed positions in one person. Which is why we need to move on from thinking of Christ as Jesus' last name and instead regard it as a designation of His three elected offices. For us to understand His roles, we'll need to look more deeply at what each of these offices entails.

Christ as Prophet

In fulfilling the role of prophet, Jesus is a proclaimer of the future and a spokesperson for God. Why is that important? Primarily because of the way Jesus presented what He had to say. The prophets prior to Jesus began their messages with this phrase: "Thus says the Lord." But when Jesus spoke God's words, He simply said, "I say to you…"

All the previous prophets were merely articulating what God had told them to tell the people. Yet when Jesus spoke, He spoke with the authority of God. After all, He is God, so this makes perfect sense. In John 1:1 we read, "In the beginning was the Word, and the Word was with God, and the Word was God." This passage lets us know that the reason Jesus could speak with authority was because when He spoke, it was actually God doing the talking.

Hebrews 1:1-2 tells us something similar: "God, after He spoke long ago to the fathers in the prophets in many portions and in many ways, in these last days has spoken to us in His Son, whom He appointed heir of all things, through whom also He made the world." Thus, Jesus Christ, in His prophetic role, is the last word on any and every subject matter. He has the final say-so on everything. You name the subject, and whatever it is, Jesus has the final word on it.

The problem in many of our lives today is that the one chosen and anointed to have the final say, Christ, is not allowed to be the last word on every subject. His words only inform ours to the degree that they agree with ours. When they differ, most of us resort to our own thoughts instead. But what Jesus has to say is the truth on every matter. His is the last word on the definition of marriage. His is the final say on when life actually begins. He has the truth about what government should do and how it ought to be defined. He defines justice, righteousness, and gender. Whatever the subject, what Jesus said goes. Christ is the prophetic statement of God Himself.

What that means is when we mix any other words with Christ's Word, we are canceling out the truth of His Word. To revisit our sin illustration from chapter 4, it's like adding a teaspoon of arsenic to a pot of stew. The entire stew is ruined. Untruth muddles truth to such a degree that the entirety of it becomes untrue as well. Christ is the beginning and end of all truth. He even knows the beginning from the end. His wisdom rules over all and ought to inform and influence us completely. You and I can save ourselves a significant amount of frustration in our lives if we will simply learn how to approach everything with one simple question, "What did Jesus say?"

Rather than viewing what Jesus said as a point in a debate and deciding whether or not we want to agree with it, we must recognize that He is the voice of God because He is the one who has been anointed as our prophet to speak for God.

Christ as Priest

Not only is Jesus anointed as prophet, but He is also anointed as priest. As such, He fulfills the role of mediator and is our access to reach God. We studied His role as the Great High Priest in chapter 5, but let's reexamine the context here. We see this role of Jesus laid out for us in multiple places in Scripture.

- *John 14:6*—"Jesus said to him, 'I am the way, and

the truth, and the life; no one comes to the Father but through Me.'"

- *1 Timothy 2:5*—"There is one God, and one mediator also between God and men, the man Christ Jesus."

- *Hebrews 2:17-18*—"He had to be made like His brethren in all things, so that He might become a merciful and faithful high priest in things pertaining to God, to make propitiation for the sins of the people. For since He Himself was tempted in that which He has suffered, He is able to come to the aid of those who are tempted."

- *Hebrews 4:14-16*—"Since we have a great high priest who has passed through the heavens, Jesus the Son of God, let us hold fast our confession. For we do not have a high priest who cannot sympathize with our weaknesses, but One who has been tempted in all things as we are, yet without sin. Therefore let us draw near with confidence to the throne of grace, so that we may receive mercy and find grace to help in time of need."

- *Hebrews 5:10*—"Being designated by God as a high priest according to the order of Melchizedek."

A lot of people will use the name God and leave out Jesus or Christ. But the problem is that Jesus fulfills the role of priest, which gives us access to God. If you skip Jesus, you sabotage your own access to God. He is the mechanism through which sinful humanity connects to a holy God. Only the sacrifice who bore our sins can bring God and humanity together.

Christ is a high priest who can understand how we feel as well. He can sympathize with our weaknesses. While God the Father knows everything, He has not felt everything. In other words, He knows things that He has never experienced.

Yet because the Father wanted to experience all, He sent His Son to earth as a man. Jesus understands loneliness. He knows what pain feels like. He comprehends emotions evoked by rejection. He even experienced death—both the death of those He loved and His own. In fact, there is no category of your life the anointed priest has not already experienced. That's why He can have compassion and mercy on you and me.

The Father can understand our pain, but the Son can empathize with it because He went through it. This can be compared to a male doctor delivering a baby versus a midwife who has given birth herself. One understands. The other understands and sympathizes. The midwife comforts as well as directs and provides help in times of need. This is what Jesus does for each one of us. He is a compassionate help when we need Him the most (Hebrews 4:15-16).

Christ as King

The third area where Christ is anointed is in the office of king. For example, King David was anointed as the ruler over Israel. He was the government itself. He was the head of all rule (see 2 Samuel 2:4; 5:3). But now that Christ has come, He is the ruler and King over all. Revelation 11:15 says, "Then the seventh angel sounded; and there were loud voices in heaven, saying, 'The kingdom of the world has become the kingdom of our Lord and of His Christ; and He will reign forever and ever.'"

In Ephesians 1:10 we read, "With a view to an administration suitable to the fullness of the times, that is, the summing up of all things in Christ, things in the heavens and things on the earth." And John 18:36-37 says...

> Jesus answered, "My kingdom is not of this world. If My kingdom were of this world, then My servants would be fighting so that I would not be handed over to the Jews; but as it is, My kingdom is not of this realm." Therefore Pilate said to Him, "So You are a king?" Jesus answered, "You say correctly that I am a king. For this I have been born, and for this I have come into the world, to testify to the truth. Everyone who is of the truth hears My voice."

Christ holds the official, appointed office as ruler over all.

Now, unfortunately, a lot of Christians relate to Christ similarly to how a lot of American citizens relate to the role of president. You will often hear Americans say things like, "Well, he may be the president, but he's not my president." They'll say this because they didn't vote for him, or because they don't agree with his temperament or policies. Essentially, they are making it known that although he may hold the position, they will not allow that position to rule over them.

And while people may not publicly say this about Christ, they infer it with their actions. Their actions proclaim, "He may be the King, but He's not king over me. He may be on

the throne, but I'm not going to let Him tell me what to do."
When those are the underlying thoughts of a person's life, that
person is living at odds with the anointed role of Christ. Christ
is the anointed King, but if He is not allowed to rule in your
decision making, ideology, career, finances, and relationships,
then you may be calling Him by His title without function-
ally allowing Him to carry out His position.

This is why I chose to place this chapter on Christ in part
2, looking at the "Power in His Person." It is true that the
name Christ refers to the distinct roles of prophet, priest, and
king. But since we are each members of His body, the church
(1 Corinthians 12:27), our right relationship to Him as a person ensures that the benefits of His roles will be carried out.
Time and again in Scripture we read of Christ in intimate ways.

- *Romans 15:7*—"Accept one another, just as Christ
  also accepted us to the glory of God."

- *Galatians 3:27*—"All of you who were baptized
  into Christ have clothed yourselves with Christ."

- *Colossians 1:26-27*—"The mystery which has been
  hidden from the past ages and generations, but has
  now been manifested to His saints, to whom God
  willed to make known what is the riches of the
  glory of this mystery among the Gentiles, which is
  Christ in you, the hope of glory."

- *Colossians 3:3*—"You have died and your life is
  hidden with Christ in God."

And in one of the most intimate, vulnerable passages in

Scripture, we read of Paul's deep longing to know Christ as much as he possibly could. The reason he wanted to know Christ was that in knowing Him, he might gain Christ by then knowing Him even more. A portion of this passage says...

> Whatever things were gain to me, those things I have counted as loss for the sake of Christ. More than that, I count all things to be loss in view of the surpassing value of knowing Christ Jesus my Lord, for whom I have suffered the loss of all things, and count them but rubbish so that I may gain Christ (Philippians 3:7-8).

Our hope is rooted in Christ, and we are hidden in Christ, accepted by Christ, and clothed in Christ. To know Christ personally and relationally is to gain access to all Christ embodies for us.

Conversely, any rejection of Christ results in a rejection of the benefits and blessings He provides through His three anointed roles. You only experience the good Christ has for you when you allow Him to fully operate through those roles in your life. You receive His provision, power, and blessings to the degree that you align yourself under and abide with His person.

Anointed

My favorite verse in the Bible sheds light on how we experience the goodness of Christ.

> I have been crucified with Christ; and it is no longer I who live, but Christ lives in me; and the life which I now live in the flesh I live by faith in the

Son of God, who loved me and gave Himself up
for me (Galatians 2:20).

Memorize this verse. Meditate on this verse. It is the key to victory in all areas of your life.

When we break down this verse, we see that what we have been crucified with is the anointing itself. We have been crucified with the three anointed offices of prophet, priest, and king—as well as what those offices stand for and produce. Likewise, when Paul says that Christ lives in us, he is referring to the anointing. The prophet, priest, and king lives in each of us.

To have Christ in you is to have all three offices within you as well. You are no longer to live on your own. Rather, you are now living according to the person who carries out these three offices perfectly.

Let me explain it through a cup of coffee. When I have my morning coffee, it starts out black. But it isn't too long before I add some sugar and cream. It's still coffee with all of that added, but it is now transformed coffee. It no longer looks the way it did when it was originally poured. The dark is now lighter. The bitter is now sweeter. I still have coffee, but it's been merged with other things.

When you and I have union with Christ personally and relationally, we are still who we were in our original fallen state, but we have now been stirred with the person of Christ. We have now added to us His transforming presence. We have everything that the three roles of prophet, priest, and king gained for us through union with Christ. But it is only to the degree that we allow Christ to live in us and make His presence known through us that we will access all He has for us in these three roles.

You have to give Christ permission to let His anointing flow through you. How do you do that? By faith in the Son of God. By tapping into His truth and applying His rule, forgiveness, standard, and Word over every part of your life. By boldly approaching the throne of grace, knowing that no sin is too large to keep you from the presence of God, because within you is the mediating power of the Great High Priest. He is both your ruler and the overruler of circumstances and challenges in your life.

Living by faith in the Son of God requires letting go of living by the flesh. You can no longer operate based on confidence in your own self, thoughts, and abilities. The way you access heaven's power and get it to fully operate in your life is through a complete reliance on and obedience to Christ. Be yoked with Christ (Matthew 11:29-30). It is He who must work for you. Yes, you have talents. Yes, you have discernment. Yes, you have effort. But none of that will amount to anything long lasting apart from the overarching rule, power, and involvement of Christ. It is He who is to speak through you as prophet. It is He who is to bring you mercy and confidence as you boldly enter the presence of the Father because He is the priest. It is He who will instruct you on what you are to do because He rules over you as King. To the degree that you rely on and remain in union with Christ is the same degree to which you will access His benefits and rewards in this life and the next.

Relying on Christ and resting in Christ for all things is the greatest life strategy you could ever apply. The closer you draw to Him and the more you allow His Words to become your own, the more you will experience the fulfillment of the purpose for which you were placed here on earth. Your life should flow with the anointing of Christ. And it will when you allow Him to be your final word, your mediating priest, and your ruler.

Paul told us how to do that in Galatians 2:20: "The life which I now live in the flesh I live by faith in the Son of God." You do it "by faith." You do it by knowing that everything you do is done by Christ through you. It is Christ who must and will work through you. He has to speak through you. He has to handle things for you. He has to walk with you through the situations that plague you. Leaning on Christ and tapping into His person enables Him to do that for you.

One Olympic sport is known as high jumping. High jumpers use their legs and jump as high as they can to clear a bar. Great high jumpers can get higher than seven feet—which is pretty high when you think about it.

But then there is another sport called pole vaulting. Now, a pole vaulter runs with a long pole in their hands, and then they stick the pole in the ground in order to clear a much higher bar. Pole vaulters can jump well over twice as high as any high jumper. Some have even surpassed 19 feet.

Now, both high jumpers and pole vaulters are trying to do the same thing. They are trying to get over a high bar. But one is doing it in their own human effort. The other is leaning on something else to propel them farther than they could go on their own—and they go so much higher.

You may be able to get so far on your own without leaning on God and yoking with Him. But it won't be very far. Eternity will reveal that. Yet when you tap into the anointing—when you grab the pole of the prophet, priest, and king—you will be able to do more than you ever even dreamed. You will see how you can love people you never liked. You can be kind when you would normally be mean. You can control your sexual urges and what you say. You can manage your emotions when you would normally lose it. You can identify your purpose and pursue your calling.

When you get propelled by the anointing working both in and through you, you will find the ability to go above and beyond what you ever thought you could in your humanity. Why? Because He is the Christ, and if you have placed your faith in Him, He is more than enough to take you higher than you ever dreamed.

Truly, truly, I say to you, you will see the heavens opened and the angels of God ascending and descending on the Son of Man.

JOHN 1:51

Truly this was the Son of God!

MATTHEW 27:54

11

SON OF GOD, SON OF MAN

I n the church where I pastor, we have who we call "sons of the ministry." These are not my biological children, of course. These men have been ordained by our church to relocate and minister elsewhere. They have come up through our discipleship programs, have experienced personal mentoring, and have grown to such a level that they are ready to fulfill the role of minister on their own. It's always exciting for me to see what the sons of the ministry go and do for the Lord. You may have heard of a few of them as they have gone on to have a national impact, such as Eric Mason.

I'm sure Paul felt the same enthusiasm when he witnessed those under him mature to such a degree that they could minister on their own as well. Paul called Timothy a son in the ministry (1 Timothy 1:2,18). Timothy was not Paul's biological son, but he was his ministerial son.

When we refer to Jesus' next names that we are going to study together, we are referring to a person who carried out two distinctly ordained roles. Jesus is both the Son of God and the Son of Man. He not only possesses the natures of both God and man, but He is also anointed to fulfill a designated role on behalf of both God and us. He can fulfill both in one person because that one person has both natures operating inside Him.

Jesus reveals the heart, goals, character, attributes, and desires of God to us (John 14:7-11; Hebrews 1:1-3). But He also identifies with our heart, goals, character, attributes, and desires as humans. He can do this because He has both the divine and human natures in Him, unmixed. This is why He could be hungry one moment, but the next moment feed 5,000 people. He could be thirsty one moment, and the next moment walk on water. One moment He could die. Then, in another moment, He could rise from the dead. This is the great dichotomy of Jesus' existence. He is both the Son of God and the Son of Man.

For Jesus to possess a divine nature means He possesses divine attributes. Thus, all that is true about God is also true about Jesus. God is omnipotent, omnipresent, omniscient, full of grace, mercy, justice, and wrath. All the characteristics that define the heart of God also define Jesus.

Yet not only is Jesus the Son of God—He is also the Son of Man. As the Son of Man on earth, Jesus got tired and hungry. He had a favorite food; He needed sleep; He cried when

His emotions led Him to do so. He was even tempted by the devil. Everything that makes us *people*, Jesus possessed in His humanity, apart from sin.

But how could Jesus be fully God, bearing all the attributes of deity, and at the same time be fully man, bearing all the attributes of humanity? The answer to that question is found in the virgin birth. We discussed the virgin birth in the opening chapter of this book, so we won't revisit it here in great detail. But there is an aspect of this birth I want you to consider more fully.

To refresh your memory: Mary's humanity came together with God's deity to create the most unique person ever to enter into human history. And while Mary was human and her DNA contained the sinful human nature, it was the role of the Holy Spirit to not only merge in her to create human life but also to protect Jesus' human nature from receiving the sin nature (Luke 1:35). This resulted in Jesus' perfect duality, which was necessary for Him to carry out the unique prophetic plan of atonement God set in place following the fall of Adam.

This plan was unique in many ways, beginning with the conception itself. After all, it was prophesied that it would be the woman's "seed" that would crush the head of the devil (Genesis 3:15). In that prophecy, God revealed early on that His method for bridging the gap created by sin would be satisfied by a human resulting from the seed of a woman.

As noted in the last chapter, this prophecy seems to have a biological contradiction inherent within it. After all, the seed of a man impregnates a woman. Never does the seed of a woman create new life.

Except in the case of Jesus.

Because in the case of Jesus, God knew in advance that the one He was talking about would not have a human father. He provided Mary with the seed, merged with the Holy Spirit, to birth the one who would crush the head of the devil. The deity of heaven produced the Son of God and the Son of Man through the woman. He produced the one who would not only reclaim what the devil had stolen from humanity when Adam sinned, but who would also possess the ability to reclaim anything and everything the devil continues to steal from anyone who is covered under the covenant of Christ (John 10:10).

How Jesus Frees You

One of the Scripture passages I love the most uncovers the purpose of this unique combination.

> Since the children share in flesh and blood, He Himself likewise also partook of the same, that through death He might render powerless him who had the power of death, that is, the devil, and might free those who through fear of death were subject to slavery all their lives (Hebrews 2:14-15).

Jesus partook of who we are in order to free who we are from what had overtaken us—not only from the literal experience, but also from the fear of it. He did this by becoming human.

God took on the flesh of a man because only the flesh can die. You can't kill a spirit. The reason He had to die was to render powerless the authority of the devil and to free us all in order to fulfill the purposes He had in creating us and placing us on earth.

Jesus died so that Satan would have no more rightful claims on those who place their faith in Him for the forgiveness of sins. Which means that if the devil still seems to have a claim on you, either you are not saved or you don't understand what it means to live daily in the regenerating, saving power Christ's atonement provides. The reason Jesus died and rose again was to remove the handcuffs off all of us, taking away the key from the devil, who held humanity hostage.

In fact, the only way believers remain incarcerated by the devil is through trickery and deception. It is in those times when Satan makes you think you are not free that you do not function freely. Satan holds countless numbers of people hostage this way, which is one reason why he is so opposed to believers growing in their knowledge and application of the Word. Because it is in the Word that you discover the truth, which will set you free (John 8:31-32). It is in the Word that you discover the breadth and scope of Jesus' salvation.

Most of us have too limited a view of Jesus' death. The majority believe that God became a man to take us to heaven.

Period.

But Jesus came, lived, breathed, died, and rose to do much more than that. Yes, He did come so you would have a way to heaven, but He also died and rose in order to bring heaven (its rule, authority, power, grace, confidence, compassion, wisdom, and more) to you on earth. Jesus came to render powerless the authority of the devil. All the devil can do now is deceive you. He doesn't rule you anymore. This is very good news!

But Jesus didn't secure your victory only for your sake. You are saved on earth from the authority of the devil so you can live out God's kingdom purpose for you. God has a divine destiny He has given you to fulfill. You have a reason for being, and that reason is significant. Far too many believers never live out their destinies because they fail to make the connection between salvation in time with God's purpose for that time.

Your life was never meant to be only about you.

You are to use your time, talents, and treasures to strategically advance God's kingdom on earth for His glory, your good, and others' benefit. Just as Jesus possessed a dual purpose as Son of God and Son of Man, once you become a follower of Jesus, you also have a dual focus. You are to set your thoughts on things above (Colossians 3:2)—preparing and planning for rewards in eternity—while also advancing the will of God on earth (Matthew 6:10).

Not only that, but when you accepted Jesus, the person and work of the Holy Spirit through Christ came into you, giving you power over sin. And since the Son of Man knew no sin, He can instruct and guide you on how to be the person you were created to be. He can give you the power to overcome sin and reverse its consequences so you can live life fully, freely, and purely in Him.

Sin has messed up all of us. Even the very presence of sin creates chaos. But in Jesus, His dual nature supplies each of us with the ability to withstand temptation and remove sin's grip on our life.

This dual nature of Jesus also opens the pathway for us to know God the Father in a more intimate manner, like He did. As the Son of God and the Son of Man, Jesus' relationship with God while on earth reflected what ours can be. He modeled a level of closeness that is open to each of us. Jesus and God remained so familiar with each other while Jesus was on earth that Jesus called Him "Father." Jesus chose to address Him by the one name that represented the natural affinity of a familial bond time and time again.

But it's interesting to note that one time He did refer to the Father as "God" when He was on the cross. As the presence of all our sin encased Him, God's holiness withdrew from the intimacy Jesus always knew. In Matthew 27:46, He uttered these words: "My God, My God, why have You forsaken Me?"

In this moment, as Jesus was dying on the cross for our sins, He didn't refer to God as Father. He couldn't locate the relationship that had once been so near. The fellowship that was there all along had been broken because of the sin of the world which Jesus bore. The one He knew as Daddy quickly became the great, looming deity we know as God. This is exactly what the presence of sin will do. Sin separates us from intimacy with God the Father. As Isaiah 59:2 puts it, "Your iniquities have made a separation between you and your God, and your sins have hidden His face from you so that He does not hear."

Sin always brings about a separation. But the closer you get to Jesus (who is your eternal and temporal salvation for sin), the closer you will get to God. In fact, as you draw nearer to Jesus, you will soon come to know God on the level of "Daddy" too.

Yet the converse of that is true as well. The further you remain from Jesus, the further you are from God as sin separates you from His presence. The relational closeness of the good Father only appears when the issue of sin has been addressed. When sin is allowed to remain in the picture, God remains the great, looming, distant deity in the sky—Creator of the heavens and earth. But once you get to know the names Son of God and Son of Man and apply the reality of their truth in your life, you gain the ability to draw close to God in a way only the atonement of a sinless Savior could allow. As Galatians 4:6 puts it, "Because you are sons, God has sent forth the Spirit of His Son into our hearts, crying, 'Abba! Father!'" Through Jesus (Son of God and Son of Man), you can experience God as Father.

The reason why many of us have not discovered more of God's presence in our lives is because we only know Him as God. He hasn't become Daddy yet. We have not come to know Him as our dear Father through the work of the God-man.

Back up a couple verses from the one we just looked at in Galatians, and you'll discover the context for calling God your Father. "When the fullness of the time came, God sent forth His Son, born of a woman, born under the Law, so that He might redeem those who were under the Law, that we might receive the adoption as sons" (verses 4-5). Through Jesus, we have been adopted by God so that He is legally our Father. God does not desire that Jesus be an only Son. Jesus is a unique child, yes. He's a one-of-a-kind Son, no doubt. But He's not the only child of God. As we draw near to Jesus and allow God's will to work in and through our lives, we become conformed to the image of Jesus and reflect Him as children of God (Romans 8:28-29).

Experiencing Greater Things

Once you recognize Jesus as the Son of God and come to believe in Him as a reflection of God Himself, you will gain access to the authority over all you need in your life on earth. The theology behind this statement is revealed to us in the story of Jesus, Philip, and Nathanael.

> The next day He purposed to go into Galilee, and He found Philip. And Jesus said to him, "Follow Me." Now Philip was from Bethsaida, of the city of Andrew and Peter. Philip found Nathanael and said to him, "We have found Him of whom Moses in the Law and also the Prophets wrote— Jesus of Nazareth, the son of Joseph." Nathanael said to him, "Can any good thing come out of Nazareth?" Philip said to him, "Come and see." Jesus saw Nathanael coming to Him, and said of him, "Behold, an Israelite indeed, in whom there is no deceit!" Nathanael said to Him, "How do You know me?" Jesus answered and said to him, "Before Philip called you, when you were under the fig tree, I saw you." Nathanael answered Him, "Rabbi, You are the Son of God; You are the King of Israel." Jesus answered and said to him, "Because I said to you that I saw you under the fig tree, do you believe? You will see greater things than these." And He said to him, "Truly, truly, I say to you, you will see the heavens opened and

the angels of God ascending and descending on the Son of Man" (John 1:43-51).

This story involves Jesus locating both Philip and Nathanael. Jesus first identified Philip, who then went and shared with Nathanael that they had found the one prophesied to serve as their King, as foretold in Daniel 7:13-14:

> I kept looking in the night visions, and behold, with the clouds of heaven One like a Son of Man was coming, and He came up to the Ancient of Days and was presented before Him. And to Him was given dominion, glory and a kingdom, that all the peoples, nations and men of every language might serve Him. His dominion is an everlasting dominion which will not pass away; and His kingdom is one which will not be destroyed.

Nathanael believed Philip's words and the prophecy, so he made his way to meet Jesus himself. However, when he met Jesus, Jesus spoke to him as if He already knew him. This took Nathanael by surprise, so he asked Jesus if He already knew him. To which Jesus explained He had seen him under the fig tree before Philip had even called him to come. He said He also knew Nathanael was a man without deceit.

Keep in mind, this was before smartphones and Face-Time. This was before Facebook Live or check-ins on Facebook. Nathanael knew there was no way for Jesus to have seen him under that fig tree apart from a supernatural work of God

Himself. When Nathanael heard this, he instantly believed. And because of his belief, Jesus informed him he would get to see even greater things than that.

While the fig tree is important to understanding this personal exchange, the fact that Jesus said he was a man without deceit is even more critical. The reason is found in Genesis 28:10-17, where we see another man who dreamed about a ladder coming down from heaven, with angels descending and ascending on this ladder. This man's name was Jacob. And Jacob was full of deceit (Genesis 25:19-34; 27:1-36).

Jesus introduced Nathanael as having the opposite character of the deceitful man who had experienced that unique closeness with heaven itself and the angelic world. As a result, Jesus blessed Nathanael with his own promise. He told Nathanael that he would "see the heavens opened and the angels of God ascending and descending on the Son of Man" (John 1:51).

Nathanael's faith in the Son of God opened up his experience with the Son of Man. It was in identifying Jesus as deity itself that Nathanael was promised the power to know Jesus and His authority on earth as well.

Far too many of us have this backward. We want the Jesus who sympathizes with our hurts or the "friend who sticks closer than a brother" (Proverbs 18:24). We want the Jesus who can heal sickness and mend hearts. But it wasn't until Nathanael first recognized the authority and awesomeness of Jesus as the Son of God that he was told he would come to know the power and presence of the Son of Man.

You might be waiting for heaven to open up. You might be waiting to experience the power of Jesus that you read about, sing about, and hear preached to you. You want to see God for yourself. You don't want Him to only be real far off in the heavenlies; you also want Him to be real right here in your realities. And God will be that for you—He will send His angels to you (Hebrews 1:14)—but only when you first honor and acknowledge Jesus as God. He is the Son of God, the exact reflection of God Himself.

When you remain in God's will, you get to see heaven open up and deliver greater things than you could ever imagine. But if you choose not to relate to Jesus in your daily life, not to honor and know Him as the Son of God, you will never benefit from His gifts to you as the Son of Man.

This promise didn't only apply to Nathanael. In fact, when we look at the original Greek for this passage, we see that Jesus used a plural form of *you* when He said, "You will see the heavens opened and the angels of God ascending and descending on the Son of Man" (John 1:51). Thus, He was not only talking to Nathanael. He was talking to all of us who recognize Him as the true Son of God.

That reality ought to make you smile. It ought to bring you encouragement. It ought to make you jump up and down and shout! Why? Because that truth promises provision for you to fully live out God's will due to your recognition of the Son of God. It gives you insight into gaining all you need, not only to live your life, but to maximize its use, fulfillment, and significance in the kingdom.

Jesus spoke of these "greater things" to Nathanael and all of us, and then went on to demonstrate an example in the very next chapter. In John 2, we read of the wedding celebration where Jesus turned the water into wine. In biblical culture, weddings lasted for a number of days, and wine was a form of bringing happiness and fun to the entire celebration. Most of the time, the hosts would give the best wine first, because that was when everyone would be able to taste it fully. Once the merriment had set in a little too much, the cheaper wine could be poured.

But at this particular wedding, the wine ran out altogether. Mary called on Jesus to save the situation and demonstrate His power to everyone there. No doubt she wanted to delight in who she knew her son to be. And while Jesus originally resisted her request, He did go on to ultimately fulfill it. Telling the servants to get empty barrels and fill them with water, Jesus then transformed the water into wine.

The headwaiter then told the bridegroom that in every wedding, they put the best wine out first, but he had served his best wine last. Jesus doesn't know how to do anything less than best!

Yet we will not get to experience the practical, tangible, and earthbound realities of Jesus' power if we fail to fully recognize Him as the Son of God. Instead of retrieving the water if that's what He tells us to do, we argue and complain that we are out of wine. We consider His direction too illogical to obey. So we don't. But the only reason the miracle at the wedding happened at all was because the servants went and filled the empty barrels like Jesus instructed.

If you are not willing to align your thoughts, words, and actions under the divinely directive rule of Jesus Christ, the Son of God, you will never experience the greater things the

Son of Man is able to do for you. It comes down to alignment. Obedience. Faith. It is entirely up to you.

I know you might be tired. I know you might be drained. You may even feel empty, like the barrels at the wedding. You look around you and see no cause for celebration. You find no happiness. No peace. No victory. No deliverance. No gain. But it is not because the Son of Man is unable to give you all these things and more. Rather, it is because you have not retrieved the water. You have not done what He has asked you to do. You're choosing to wait for your miracle rather than work for your miracle. Your work involves obedience to Jesus as the Son of God.

Yet if you decide to do as He says, you will see heaven open up and the angels of God ascending and descending on the Son of Man. You will see heaven's intervention in history. Jesus is both the Son of God and the Son of Man, connecting heaven with earth and providing you with all you need to live out your divine destiny.

In the beginning was the Word, and the Word was with God, and the Word was God...And the Word became flesh, and dwelt among us, and we saw His glory, glory as of the only begotten of the Father, full of grace and truth.

JOHN 1:1,14

God, after He spoke long ago to the fathers in the prophets in many portions and in many ways, in these last days has spoken to us in His Son, whom He appointed heir of all things, through whom also He made the world.

HEBREWS 1:1-2

12

WORD

Where did everything come from?
This is not just an abstract question, but one that has a profound effect on each of our lives. Your belief about the origin of the world affects the way you think about your life, your choices, and your values.

Some would have us believe that at the very beginning there was basically *nothing*, then suddenly, following a big bang, there was *something*. That *something* involved the particles that make up the building blocks of life. These, over the process of billions of years, evolved into everything we see today, including you and me.

Frankly, I think it takes a lot of faith to believe in a scenario like that, especially since there isn't really any solid evidence behind this story. In fact, I think it takes more faith to believe in evolution than to believe the creation story the Bible tells.

And the theory of evolution itself keeps evolving as people

hunt for scientific evidence to support it. At its core, the theory suggests that God isn't necessary. That something came from nothing, and order came from chaos. That an impersonal process lies behind everything in our world.

When we remove God from the equation, we are left without meaning and without purpose. Perhaps the appeal of the evolutionary theory for many people is that it also dismisses our sense of accountability to a personal God who made us.

Is the cause of everything just a primordial explosion of highly compressed matter? And does that explosion then explode our sense of responsibility to God? Do people believe in this theory because they are convinced it is true, or because it lets them off the hook from answering for their lives and actions? Evolution can be used as an opportunity to deny our accountability to God. It can suggest that we don't have to answer to anyone, because there is no thinking, personal being who is bigger than us and can override our decisions. Evolution lets us believe we are our own god.

But the Bible tells a different story.

The Word and Creation

When John 1:1 speaks about the beginning of time, it reminds us that Jesus was there at the very first moment of creation. The Bible's account of creation is not about an accident occurring because of a big bang, but about intentionality and purpose and involvement. Jesus is there on page one of history. Though He doesn't show up in His incarnate (human) form until well after the close of the Old Testament, He's been on the scene since before the curtains even opened. We get a glimpse of this when looking at the following verses.

- *Revelation 19:13*—"He is clothed with a robe dipped in blood, and His name is called The Word of God."

- *John 1:1*—"In the beginning was the Word, and the Word was with God, and the Word was God."

Thus, we see that one of the names of Jesus in the Bible is the Word of God. The Greek translation of *word* is *logos*. *Logos* was a very powerful word in the day that Jesus lived. The reason it was so powerful was because the Greeks used that word to define the impersonal force behind the universe. When the Greeks spoke about the logos, it was in the context of identifying a creative force that gave rise to all knowledge, wisdom, and even creation. In order to understand the culture at that time, a person would need to be familiar with the term *logos*.

Thus, when John wrote his epistle, he drew on an existing term already packed with meaning and infused it with additional meaning. He took a word his contemporary culture already understood as representing a powerful force behind all creation—and then injected it with the truth. Like any great writer or speaker, when he sought to emphasize the word *logos*, he repeated it from a variety of angles. "In the beginning was the Word, and the Word was with God, and the Word was God…And the Word became flesh" (John 1:1,14).

John begins by telling us that the Word was the start of all things. In fact, He existed before the start of all known things. We know this because John uses the past tense *was* and not *is* when he introduces the Word. The Word preceded the beginning, and in so doing preexisted the existence of everything else.

The second thing John points out to us is that the Word not only preexisted, but also coexisted. "The Word was with God." The Greek term translated *with* in this passage means "face to face." It refers to a high level of communication with God. They looked into each other's eyes, so to speak. Stared at each other. Closely communed with each other. Were in alignment with each other.

Thirdly, John tells us that the Word was God. By this we see that this preexistent, coexistent Word was also self-existent, because God is the only one who does not need anything outside Himself in order to be Himself. Nothing else in creation can exist without being dependent on something else. God alone is self-contained.

Lastly, John tells us that the Word became flesh. He was preexistent, coexistent, and self-existent, but He also became tangibly existent. God introduced the physical manifestation of His rule and divinity into the creation which He Himself had made.

The word *word* can take on many meanings, especially having to do with communication—like when someone says to you, "I'd like to have a word with you." When we speak a word with someone or to someone, we are saying things to them. In that same vein, the Word exists as the communication channel between God and humanity. In Psalm 138:2 we read, "I will bow down toward Your holy temple and give thanks to Your name for Your lovingkindness and Your truth; for You have magnified Your word according to all Your name."

Whenever we see the name Word in Scripture, it references both the message of God and a person. The meaning extends beyond the communication from God's mouth and reaches into the very existence of His life. The Word is more than spoken content, although it includes that definition—it also references the very nature of the speaker Himself.

God's Word is equal to God's person since the Word was God. The Word *is* God.

Friend, the Word has a history. He existed prior to the beginning. And the only thing that precedes the beginning is eternity. The Word was intimately face-to-face with God. In fact, it *was* God. So when we talk about the Word, we are talking about the self-revelation of God. The Word is not an impersonal force. John used the pronoun *He*, not *it*, when discussing the Word in John 1. The Word is a person, not merely a form of communication. Thus, the Word of God is not the logos of the Greeks. The Word is…

preexistent

coexistent

self-existent

tangibly existent

self-contained

self-evident

The Word is a *who*, a person comprised of much more than anyone else who ever existed. This Word is responsible for creation. As John 1:3 tells us, nothing came into being that came into being apart from the Word. We read, "All things came into being through Him, and apart from Him nothing came into being that has come into being." John 1:3 cancels out the big bang theory and the theory of evolution in their entirety. This is because they are dependent upon impersonal forces at work, not a person at work. The creation in which we live and have our being is tied to a *He*, not an *it*. Creation is tied to a person, not some scientific principle. Nothing has come into being that was not brought into being by the Word itself, who existed before the beginning with God and was God.

It isn't difficult to understand why believers in evolution willingly check their brains at the door. Because when humanity understands that a being—God Himself—created the universe, then they also understand that they are accountable. Evolution provides the opportunity to deny that. Evolution says, "I do not have to answer to anyone. There is no thinking, personal being who is bigger than me and can override my decisions." Many people want to be their own god. They want to control their own existence. So they choose to believe in an impersonal force that combusted into creation.

Much of the chaos we witness in our society today is due to a system of evolutionary thought that removes God, His standards, and His rule from humanity. Everyone has their own version of truth under evolution. We can live independent of morals, virtues, and values if we choose to dismiss the facts that God exists and that the Word (Jesus) brought about the world in which we live. This dismissal of God's overarching rule shows up in our crime rates, personal conflicts, abortion rates, definition of life, definitions of gender and sexuality, as well as the decisions about how we use our time. When we don't believe in God, we think we can determine our own truth, can run things the way we want, and are accountable to no one at all. But if we want to run our own world, we've got to make our own world, because God made this one, and He calls the shots—whether we acknowledge this or not.

Concerning the creation of this world, we read clearly:

- *Colossians 1:16-17*—"By [the Son] all things were created, both in the heavens and on earth, visible and invisible, whether thrones or dominions or rulers or authorities—all things have been created through Him and for Him. He is before all things, and in Him all things hold together."

- *Hebrews 1:1-2*—"God, after He spoke long ago to the fathers in the prophets in many portions and in many ways, in these last days has spoken to us in His Son, whom He appointed heir of all things, through whom also He made the world."

The world was made by God through Jesus and for Jesus. Contrary to popular opinion, it was not made first and foremost for us. Jesus, the Word through whom God made creation, is the reason God made it in the first place. Colossians tells us that all things were created "through Him and for Him." In fact, He holds all of it in place. So when God created the world through Jesus, He gave it back to Him as a present. Understanding ownership of creation is critical to finding peace, faith, and purpose.

The Word Is Life and Light

Genesis 1:1-3 says, "In the beginning God created the heavens and the earth. The earth was formless and void, and darkness was over the surface of the deep, and the Spirit of God was moving over the surface of the waters. Then God said, 'Let there be light'; and there was light." The word *light* in this passage is life itself. It is Christ Himself, even though it is also Christ who did the speaking as God's spokesman, the Word.

We see this in John 1:4-5, where it says of Jesus, "In Him was life, and the life was the Light of men. The Light shines in the darkness, and the darkness did not comprehend it." Jesus is the light—the life—that He spoke into creation. He is in all and over all (Ephesians 4:6).

How does all of this apply to the discussion on evolution that opened this chapter? Well, the creationist view of the beginning of time also requires faith, sure. But creationists believe that life produced life. They believe in someone who is alive and who made other things alive too. A living God produced living plants, living animals, living people, and the entire cycle of life itself. But in the evolutionary theory, the belief rests in impersonal matter creating very personal and ordered life.

Both belief systems require faith. Yet one is faith in a living being. The other is faith in combustible matter.

As you come to know Jesus according to the name Word, you come face-to-face with His creative and life-giving power. We don't often associate these attributes to Jesus. Somehow we have this notion that God created and ran everything for Himself, and then Jesus showed up centuries later. But this name reveals a different history entirely. This name places Jesus not only as an active participant in the creation process, but also as the very reason creation was made. He is the giver and receiver of life.

To apply this attribute of Jesus to your own life, you must first understand that this name animates life. By tapping into the Word, you tap into the source and purpose of life.

We saw that "in Him was life" (John 1:4). The very definition of life is in Jesus. Thus, a person cannot define life without defining it through Jesus. Which means we can never fully live life the way it was meant to be lived without Jesus Christ. That is why Acts 17:28 says, "In Him we live and move and exist." His life is our life. Apart from Jesus, we do not have life. And in Him we are given the light we need to live, because his life is "the Light of men" (John 1:4). What does light do? It enables us to see. So in Jesus, we can see. But it might be easier to understand this idea if we reverse it: If there is no Jesus, there is no light, and people live in darkness.

That is why when someone rejects Jesus Christ and His rightful role as the one who created all and the one for whom all was created, that person walks in darkness. Rejecting Jesus means rejecting the light by which we are to live. This rejection can occur regarding salvation for nonbelievers, but it can also occur in relation to everyday life for believers. When Jesus' perspective is not brought to rule on your perspective, then you have rejected Him. When Jesus' rule is not allowed to overrule your decisions, then you have rejected Him. When Jesus' love is not allowed to flow from your heart to others, then you have rejected Him. And to reject Christ is to turn off the light. It is to stumble about in darkness. To stub your toe. Trip. Tumble. Wind up lost. And much, much more, such as suffering consequences due to sin, selfishness, and stubbornness of soul.

Light always overcomes darkness. Always. No matter how dark it is or how long it has been dark, when you light a candle or turn on a lamp, everything changes. Darkness has to flee in the face of light. Similarly, when you intentionally choose to bring Jesus' perspective, thoughts, and will into your own and let Him rule over you as Lord, His light will drive out the darkness plaguing your life. You won't have to fight it in order to drive it away—His light drives it away. He is the light, and in His light is found life.

Many Christians are functioning in spiritual darkness today because they won't let Jesus be the light in their life, decisions, or thoughts. They do not allow His Word to be the final word in their decision making. Whenever Jesus is excluded, darkness seeps in. Whenever He is excluded, darkness eventually wins. Since creation was created through Him and for Him and is held together by Him, there is nothing you touch, no place you go, and no choice you make that is not somehow tied to Him.

And yet so many believers live their lives and merely give Jesus a nod or a handshake. Then they wonder why they are unable to overcome life's challenges or discover the contentment, joy, and abundant life Christ died to provide. It's simple why they cannot: Darkness rules when the light is turned off.

Bottom line: It's all about Jesus. And when you choose not to make your life all about Jesus, you are on your own. That's why Scripture tells us, "Whether, then, you eat or drink or whatever you do, do all to the glory of God" (1 Corinthians 10:31). God made it clear that something as mundane and routine as eating is still to be done for His glory. After all, the reason you can eat is because Jesus created the food. He created your mouth. He created your digestive system. And what's more, He holds all of that together so you can function. To eat apart from acknowledging that He is both the giver and sustainer of life is to dismiss His integral role in all of life. Everything was made to boomerang glory back to Jesus.

The secret to life is simply to boomerang more and more glory back to Jesus. Because when you do, He will infuse more and more life into you and whatever it is you are doing. See, the name Word isn't merely a word. This name represents the entire reason you exist. Jesus, the Word, is the centerpiece of life. He is the provider of life and the purpose of life itself. To skip Jesus is the most personally damaging thing you could ever do.

The Word Made Flesh

We read in John 1:14 how Jesus took on flesh and "dwelt among us." The term *dwelt* in this verse means "pitched His tent." Literally, the verse reads, "The Word became flesh, and [tented] among us." A synonym for *tent* is *tabernacle*. The audience to whom John was writing would have understood what he meant when he said the Word became flesh and became a living tabernacle among them. They knew the meaning because they knew the history of the Israelites in the wilderness. They knew that a tabernacle was set up with a unique, special place within called the Holy of Holies. In this area of the tabernacle sat the Ark of the Covenant. On top of this ark were two golden cherubim that oversaw the mercy seat, where God's presence dwelt. Inside the ark rested the two tablets containing the Ten Commandments (Exodus 25:10-22).

Picture this: The glory of God was on top of the chest, while the Ten Commandments were within the chest under the mercy seat. And all this rested within the confines of the Holy of Holies in the tabernacle in the wilderness.

This is the scene John references when introducing the concept that Jesus "tented" among us. He came into a sin-soaked world, a wilderness of souls, bringing the presence of God through His own mercy. He came to bring life where life was not found. He did it for people back then, and He still does it for us today. Which is why I can say that it doesn't matter how dry your wilderness is…or how many thorns and thistles have grown in your circumstances…or how many Canaanites, Hittites, Amorites, or Jebusites have surrounded you. It doesn't matter, because a tent has been pitched right in the middle of your wilderness existence. And that tent is the Word made flesh.

Jesus walked the streets in Israel. He talked. He ate. He did all the things humans do, but He did them as the manifested Word—the revelation of God. Which is why we read in John 1:14 that we "saw His glory, glory as of the only begotten from the Father." Notice that this verse says "only begotten," which suggests He is uniquely one of a kind. There is none like Him. There has never been, nor will there ever be, another Jesus. According to Colossians 2:9, "In Him all the fullness of Deity dwells in bodily form." The fullness of God the Father resides in Jesus Christ.

Yet even though this fullness resides in Him, we learn something powerful about Him when we read Philippians 2:6-9.

> Although He existed in the form of God, [He] did not regard equality with God a thing to be grasped, but emptied Himself, taking the form of a bond-servant, and being made in the likeness of men. Being found in appearance as a man, He humbled Himself by becoming obedient to the point of death, even death on a cross. For this reason also, God highly exalted Him, and bestowed on Him the name which is above every name.

In this passage, we discover that even though Jesus was (and is) equal with God, He didn't allow His equality to keep Him from carrying out His responsibility. He recognized that He had a role to play, and He willingly carried out that role. When the passage says that Jesus "emptied Himself," the phrase comes from the Greek word *kenóō*, which means "to pour out." He completely poured out His deity into humanity and became a slave to His purpose. He became a slave to bringing us salvation. He humbled Himself to the point of death so that we could live.

This is why understanding this name of Jesus—the Word—is so critical. Because it isn't just anyone who emptied Himself out for service. No, this is the one through whom and by whom and for whom all things exist. This is the one who holds the entire world together. The source of life itself gave up His life so that we can live.

His is no small sacrifice. He didn't make it because He had nothing better to do. His is the greatest sacrifice of all time. And He gave it willingly so that He might accomplish the return of the King's rule over the hearts of mankind.

One of the reasons more Christians do not see the movement of God in their lives is because they will not allow Jesus to carry out what He accomplished. Through His life and through His death, He brought the living tabernacle to our life so we could have access to the full power of God in all we do. Yet if we only visit that living tabernacle for a few hours on Sunday or during a five-minute devotional to start our day, we will not have the light and life that we need throughout every moment of every day. What good is a flashlight tucked away in your drawer?

Jesus is the light of life, but His thoughts, perspective, heart, and intentions must be made to bear on your thoughts, perspective, heart, and intentions. Otherwise you are living in darkness and lacking access to the victory which is rightfully yours by way of the cross.

The Word is God incarnate. The Word is life. The Word is light. Like oxygen to the lungs and cells in the body, the Word has all we need to live our life abundantly. But as soon as He is removed, ignored, or dismissed, we cut off the essence of life itself. And then we wonder why things are falling apart.

It is only in the intentional, ongoing pursuit of His presence, purpose, power, and perspective through abiding in His written Word (the Bible) and with His Spirit that you will experience the fullness of life you desire. As Colossians 3:16 says, "Let the word of Christ richly dwell within you."

Pursue intimacy with Jesus through His Word, and you'll get life as part of the package (John 17:3). Because from the beginning, Jesus has been the life, light, and living manifestation of deity who sits over all, orders all, and holds all of life together.

SOMETHING ABOUT
THAT NAME

A story goes that a rich man was on his way to a bank one day when he ran across a beggar. He asked the beggar how he had wound up on the streets. The beggar explained that he had gone to college, but he had made mistakes and ruined his life, and now he had nothing. The rich man felt pity for him and wrote him a large check so he could have a chance at starting his life over again.

Yet the next week when the rich man walked to the same bank, he saw the same man sitting there begging once again. Alarmed, the rich man went over to the beggar and asked him why he was still on the streets. The beggar replied, "When I went to the bank to cash the check, they didn't believe the check was real. They took one look at my clothes and my hair, noticed how I smelled, and determined the check couldn't have been mine after all. So here I am. I guess I have no way to move forward."

The rich man immediately grabbed the hand of the beggar and walked into the bank with him. He said it didn't matter what he was wearing, how long ago he washed his hair, or how awful he smelled. The only thing that mattered was the name that had signed the check. As you might imagine, the check was cashed right away.

Friend, I don't know how messed up you may be today. I don't know how chaotic your life might feel. But I do know there is a name above every name, under which everything must bow. All demons must submit to this name. All circumstances must submit to this name. All issues must submit to this name. Because in this name is found all authority, all power, all compassion, all time, all might, all peace, and all wisdom. As the psalmist says, "O magnify the LORD with me, and let us exalt His name together" (Psalm 34:3).

Jesus' names empower and equip you to live out your life to the fullest. We have touched upon a number of these names in our time together throughout this book, but don't let this be where you stop getting to know Jesus. There are many, many more names. In fact, He is found all throughout Scripture—whether directly or indirectly. He rescues, supplies, provides, comforts, guides, gives, loves, and goes to battle for you.

In fact, there are so many names of Jesus that I had to pick only a few for us to examine together. But as we wrap up our study on Jesus' names, let's be reminded of who He is throughout the entirety of Scripture. The list below includes names and descriptive phrases that all point back to Jesus, who embodies the fullness of God Himself.

In Genesis, He is the Creator God.

In Exodus, He is the redeemer.

In Leviticus, He is your sanctification.

In Numbers, He is your guide.

In Deuteronomy, He is your teacher.

In Joshua, He is the mighty conqueror.

In Judges, He gives victory over enemies.

In Ruth, He is your kinsman, your lover, your redeemer.

In 1 Samuel, He is the root of Jesse.

In 2 Samuel, He is the Son of David.

In 1 and 2 Kings, He is King of kings and Lord of lords.

In 1 and 2 Chronicles, He is your intercessor and Great High Priest.

In Ezra, He is your temple, your house of worship.

In Nehemiah, He is your mighty wall, protecting you from your enemies.

In Esther, He stands in the gap to deliver you from your enemies.

In Job, He is the arbitrator who not only understands your struggles, but also has the power to do something about them.

In Psalms, He is your song and your reason to sing.

In Proverbs, He is your wisdom, helping you make sense of life and live it successfully.

In Ecclesiastes, He is your purpose, delivering you from vanity.

In the Song of Solomon, He is your lover, your rose of Sharon.

In Isaiah, He is the Wonderful Counselor, Mighty God, Eternal Father, and Prince of Peace. In short, He's everything you need.

In Jeremiah, He is your balm of Gilead, the soothing salve for your soul.

In Lamentations, He is the ever-faithful one upon whom you can depend.

In Ezekiel, He is the one who assures that dry, dead bones will come alive again.

In Daniel, He is the Ancient of Days, the everlasting God who never runs out of time.

In Hosea, He is your faithful lover, always beckoning you to come back—even when you have abandoned Him.

In Joel, He is your refuge, keeping you safe in times of trouble.

In Amos, He is the husbandman, the one you can depend on to stay by your side.

In Obadiah, He is Lord of the kingdom.

In Jonah, He is your salvation, bringing you back within His will.

In Micah, He is judge of the nation.

In Nahum, He is the jealous God.

In Habakkuk, He is the holy one.

In Zephaniah, He is the witness.

In Haggai, He overthrows the enemies.

In Zechariah, He is Lord of hosts.

In Malachi, He is the messenger of the covenant.

In Matthew, He is the King of the Jews.

In Mark, He is the servant.

In Luke, He is the Son of Man, feeling what you feel.

In John, He is the Son of God.

In Acts, He is the Savior of the world.

In Romans, He is the righteousness of God.

In 1 Corinthians, He is the rock that followed Israel.

In 2 Corinthians, He is the triumphant one, giving victory.

In Galatians, He is your liberty; He sets you free.

In Ephesians, He is head of the church.

In Philippians, He is your joy.

In Colossians, He is your completeness.

In 1 Thessalonians, He is your hope.

In 2 Thessalonians, He is your glory.

In 1 Timothy, He is your faith.

In 2 Timothy, He is your stability.

In Titus, He is God your Savior.

In Philemon, He is your benefactor.

In Hebrews, He is your perfection.

In James, He is the power behind your faith.

In 1 Peter, He is your example.

In 2 Peter, He is your purity.

In 1 John, He is your life.

In 2 John, He is your pattern.

In 3 John, He is your motivation.

In Jude, He is the foundation of your faith.

In Revelation, He is your coming King.

From start to finish, there is no place you can look and not discover Jesus. He is over all. He is in all. He is our all in all.

There's something awesome about the name Jesus. So make sure you wear the name through your public identification with Him, then bear the name by being willing to suffer because of your association with Him, and finally share the name as you witness to others about your Savior.

NOTES

1. Part of chapter 1 is adapted from *The Power of the Cross: Putting It to Work in Your Life* by Tony Evans (©2016). Published by Moody Publishers. Used by permission.

2. "I believe in Christianity as I believe that the Sun has risen not only because I see it but because by it I see everything else." C.S. Lewis, as quoted in "Christianity Makes Sense of the World," *Reflections*, C.S. Lewis Institute, October 26, 2013, http://www.cslewisinstitute.org/Christianity_Makes_Sense_of_the_World (October 31, 2018).

3. Parts of chapter 1 and chapter 6 are adapted from *Like No Other: The Life of Christ* by Tony Evans (©2014), pp 18-20,29. Published by Lifeway Publishers. Used by permission.

4. Some Jews practiced the act of replacing the spoken name with "Adonai" while speaking in the synagogue, as they felt "Yahweh" was too holy to be said. This is still practiced by many to this day.

5. Parts of chapter 8 are excerpted from *The Kingdom Agenda: Life Under God* by Tony Evans (©2013). Published by Moody Publishers. Used by permission.

Dr. Tony Evans
and the
Urban Alternative

About Dr. Tony Evans

Dr. Tony Evans is founder and senior pastor of the 10,000-member Oak Cliff Bible Fellowship in Dallas, founder and president of the Urban Alternative, chaplain of the NBA's Dallas Mavericks, and author of many books, including *Destiny* and *Victory in Spiritual Warfare*. His radio broadcast, *The Alternative with Dr. Tony Evans*, can be heard on more than 1,300 outlets and in more than 130 countries.

The Urban Alternative

The Urban Alternative (TUA) equips, empowers, and unites Christians to impact individuals, families, churches, and communities through a thoroughly kingdom agenda worldview. In teaching truth, we seek to transform lives.

The core cause of the problems we face in our personal lives, homes, churches, and societies is spiritual; therefore, the only way to address it is spiritually. We've tried a political, social, economic, and even a religious agenda. It's time for a kingdom agenda—the visible manifestation of the comprehensive rule of God over every area of life.

The unifying, central theme of the Bible is the glory of God and the advancement of His kingdom. This is the conjoining thread from Genesis to Revelation—from beginning to end. Without that theme, the Bible might look like disconnected stories that are inspiring but seem to be unrelated in purpose and direction. The Bible exists to share God's movement in history to establish and expand His kingdom. Understanding that increases the relevance of these ancient writings in our day-to-day living because the kingdom is not only then—it is now.

The absence of the kingdom's influence in our own lives and in our families, churches, and communities has led to a catastrophic deterioration in our world.

- People live segmented, compartmentalized lives because they lack God's kingdom worldview.

- Families disintegrate because they exist for their own satisfaction rather than for the kingdom.

- Churches have limited impact because they fail to comprehend that the goal of the church is not to advance the church itself, but the kingdom.

- Communities have nowhere to turn to find real solutions for real people who have real problems, because the church has become divided, ingrown, and powerless to transform the cultural landscape in any relevant way.

The kingdom agenda offers us a way to live with a solid hope by optimizing the solutions of heaven. When God and His rule are not the final and authoritative standard over all, order and hope are lost. But the reverse of that is true as well—as long as we have God, we have hope. If God is still in the picture, and as long as His agenda is still on the table, it's not over.

Even if relationships collapse, God will sustain you. Even if finances dwindle, God will keep you. Even if dreams die, God will revive you. As long as God and His rule guide your life, family, church, and community, there is always hope.

Our world needs the King's agenda. Our churches need the King's agenda. Our families need the King's agenda.

In many major cities, drivers can take a loop to get to the other side of the city without driving straight through downtown. This loop takes them close enough to the city to see its towering buildings and skyline, but not close enough to actually experience it.

This is precisely what our culture has done with God. We have put Him on the "loop" of our personal, family, church, and community lives. He's close enough to be at hand should we need Him in an emergency, but far enough away that He can't be the center of who we are.

Sadly, we often want God on the loop of our lives, but we don't always want the King of the Bible to come downtown into the very heart of our ways. Leaving God on the loop brings about dire consequences, as we have seen in our own lives and with others. But when we make God and His rule the centerpiece of all we think, do, and say, we experience Him in the way He longs for us to.

He wants us to be kingdom people with kingdom minds set on fulfilling His kingdom purposes. He wants us to pray as Jesus did—"Not My will, but Yours be done" (Luke 22:42)—because His is the kingdom, the power, and the glory.

There is only one God, and we are not Him. As King and Creator, God calls the shots. Only when we align ourselves underneath His comprehensive authority will we access His full power and authority in our lives, families, churches, and communities.

As we learn how to govern ourselves under God, we will transform the institutions of family, church, and society according to a biblically based, kingdom worldview. Under Him, we touch heaven and change earth.

To achieve our goal, we use a variety of strategies, approaches, and resources for reaching and equipping as many people as possible.

Broadcast Media

Millions of individuals experience *The Alternative with Dr. Tony Evans*, a daily broadcast playing on over 1,300 radio outlets and in more than 100 countries. The broadcast can also be seen on several television networks, online at tonyevans.org, and on the free Tony Evans app. More than four million message downloads occur each year.

Leadership Training

The *Tony Evans Training Center (TETC)* facilitates educational programming that embodies the ministry philosophy of Dr. Tony Evans as expressed through the kingdom agenda. The training courses focus on leadership development and discipleship in five tracks:

- Bible and theology
- personal growth
- family and relationships
- church health and leadership development
- society and community impact

Kingdom Agenda Pastors (KAP) provides a viable network for like-minded pastors who embrace the kingdom agenda philosophy. Pastors have the opportunity to go deeper with Dr. Tony Evans as they are given greater biblical knowledge, practical applications, and resources to impact individuals, families, churches, and communities. KAP welcomes senior and associate pastors of all churches. KAP also offers an annual summit, held each year in Dallas, Texas, with intensive seminars, workshops, and resources.

Pastors' Wives Ministry, founded by Dr. Lois Evans, provides counsel, encouragement, and spiritual resources for pastors' wives as they serve with their husbands in ministry. A primary focus of the ministry is the KAP Summit, which offers senior pastors' wives a safe place to reflect, renew, and relax along with training in personal development, spiritual growth, and care for their emotional and physical well-being.

Community Impact

National Church Adopt-a-School Initiative (NCAASI) empowers churches across the country to impact communities through public schools, effecting positive social change in urban youth and families. Leaders of churches, school districts, faith-based organizations, and other nonprofit organizations are equipped with the knowledge and tools to forge partnerships and build strong social service delivery systems. This training is based on the comprehensive church-based community impact strategy conducted by Oak Cliff Bible Fellowship. It addresses areas such as economic development, education, housing, health revitalization, family renewal, and racial reconciliation. NCAASI assists churches in tailoring the model to meet specific needs of their communities, while addressing the spiritual and moral frame of reference. Training events are held annually in the Dallas area at Oak Cliff Bible Fellowship.

Athlete's Impact (AI) is an outreach into and through sports. Coaches are sometimes the most influential adults in young people's lives—even more than parents. With the rise of fatherlessness in our culture, more young people are looking to their coaches for guidance, character development, practical needs, and hope. Athletes (professional or amateur) also influence younger athletes and kids. Knowing this, we equip and train coaches and athletes to live out and utilize their God-given roles for the benefit of the kingdom. We aim to do this through our iCoach App, weCoach Football Conference, and other resources, such as *The Playbook: A Life Strategy Guide for Athletes*.

Resource Development

We foster lifelong learning partnerships with the people we serve by providing a variety of published materials. Dr. Evans has published more than 100 unique titles (booklets, books, and Bible studies) based on more than 40 years of preaching.

Our goal is to strengthen individuals in their walk with God and service to others.

For more information and a complimentary copy of Dr. Evans' devotional newsletter,

call
(800) 800-3222

or write
TUA
PO Box 4000
Dallas TX 75208

or visit
www.tonyevans.org

More Great
Harvest House Books By
Dr. Tony Evans

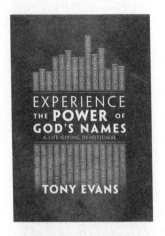

EXPERIENCE
THE **POWER** OF
GOD'S NAMES
A LIFE-GIVING DEVOTIONAL

TONY EVANS

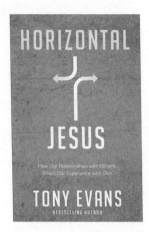

HORIZONTAL
JESUS

How Our Relationships with Others
Affect Our Experience with God

TONY EVANS
BESTSELLING AUTHOR

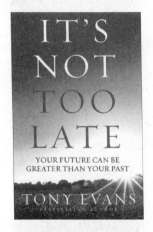

IT'S
NOT
TOO
LATE

YOUR FUTURE CAN BE
GREATER THAN YOUR PAST

TONY EVANS
BESTSELLING AUTHOR

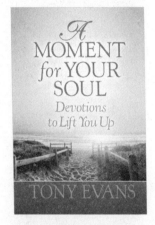

A
MOMENT
for YOUR
SOUL
Devotions
to Lift You Up

TONY EVANS

THE **POWER** OF
GOD'S NAMES

TONY EVANS
BESTSELLING AUTHOR

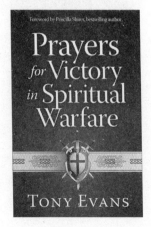

Foreword by Priscilla Shirer, bestselling author

Prayers
for Victory
in Spiritual
Warfare

TONY EVANS

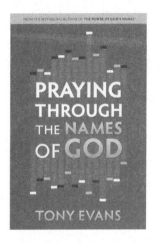

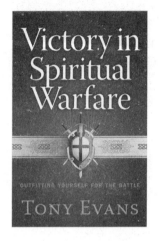

Tony EVANS
THE URBAN ALTERNATIVE

YOUR *Eternity* IS OUR *Priority*

At The Urban Alternative, eternity is our priority—for the individual, the family, the church and the nation. The 45-year teaching ministry of Tony Evans has allowed us to reach a world in need with:

The Alternative – Our flagship radio program brings hope and comfort to an audience of millions on over 1,300 radio outlets across the country.

tonyevans.org – Our library of teaching resources provides solid Bible teaching through the inspirational books and sermons of Tony Evans.

Tony Evans Training Center – Experience the adventure of God's Word with our online classroom, providing at-your-own-pace courses for your PC or mobile device.

Tony Evans app – Packed with audio and video clips, devotionals, Scripture readings and dozens of other tools, the mobile app provides inspiration on-the-go.

**Explore God's kingdom today.
Live for more than the moment.
Live for *eternity*.**

tonyevans.org

To learn more about Harvest House books and
to read sample chapters, visit our website:

www.harvesthousepublishers.com

HARVEST HOUSE PUBLISHERS
EUGENE, OREGON